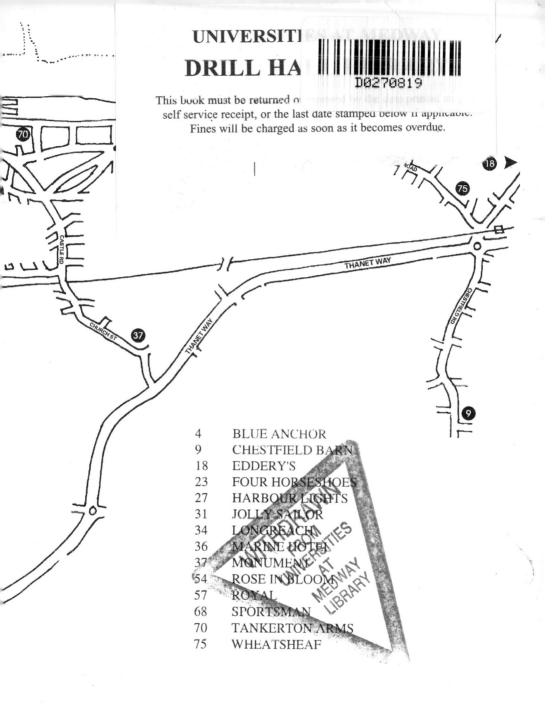

D0270819

This book must be returned o̲n̲ ̲.̲.̲.̲ ̲.̲.̲.̲ ̲.̲.̲.̲ ̲.̲.̲ printed on
self service receipt, or the last date stamped below if applicable.
Fines will be charged as soon as it becomes overdue.

4	BLUE ANCHOR
9	CHESTFIELD BARN
18	EDDERY'S
23	FOUR HORSESHOES
27	HARBOUR LIGHTS
31	JOLLY SAILOR
34	LONGREACH
36	MARINE HOTEL
37	MONUMENT
54	ROSE IN BLOOM
57	ROYAL
68	SPORTSMAN
70	TANKERTON ARMS
75	WHEATSHEAF

WITHDRAWN FROM UNIVERSITIES AT MEDWAY LIBRARY

The Cross
High Street
Whitstable.

ALES AND TALES

Pubs in the Story of Whitstable

Geoffrey Pike
Mike Page
John Cann

Old Neptune and the Swale

**Published by Whitstable Improvement Trust
at Harbour Street, Whitstable, Kent CT5 1AH.
Registered Charity No. 802040.**

First Published October 1993

Copyright © 1993
        Publication - Whitstable Improvement Trust
        Text - Geoffrey Pike & Mike Page
        Illustrations - John Cann
        Cover Photographs - Daniel Tolhurst

All rights reserved. No part of this book may be reproduced in any way without the written permission of the copyright holders.

ISBN No. 0-9515828-3-6

Project Co-ordinator - John Cann

Typesetting and layout by New Perspective, Unit 42, John Wilson Business Park, Thanet Way, Whitstable Kent CT5 4QT.

Printed by Oyster Press, Unit 74, Joseph Wilson Industrial Estate, Whitstable, Kent CT5 3PS.

UNIVERSITIES AT MEDWAY
11 MAR 2011
DRILLHALL LIBRARIES

CONTENTS

The Whitstable Improvement Trust is an independent Charitable Trust and Limited Company devoted to the careful preservation and the regeneration of Whitstable. It seeks to retain and care for the unique nature of the locality and its buildings, whilst creating an awareness of the town's historical past and the characters who have contributed to it. Initially funded by the city and county councils, the Trust now exists through its own resources and initiatives with the support of those who live and work in the town and its environs.

INTRODUCTION

Whitstable was widely famous for the quality of its oysters - the Whitstable Natives. Locally it had a great reputation for the number of its licensed premises - the haunts of other natives. In mid-Victorian times it was said a man could drink his way round town visiting a different establishment each week for a whole year: a total of 52 - and that for a population of scarcely 4,000.

The local history of many communities is often written around the parish church: its building, records and monuments being graphic illustrations of the lives and fortunes of the people and the place. However Whitstable's church was for long isolated in a hamlet away on a hill inland, while a lively community grew and expanded quite separately down by the shore.

So in this book licensed premises are the framework within which the story of Whitstable is told. From the tippling house of Tudor times to the alehouse, from the later inn and tavern to the Victorian beer-house the story moves to the modern public house and hotel.

The lives and livelihoods of the people were inextricably linked with the sea, and there is evidence of this in a number of local inn signs such as the Ship and Jolly Sailor; in particular types of boat: the Hoy, the Smack and the Steam

1

Packet, and in occupations: the Fisherman's and Dredgerman's Arms. Less obvious is the name of the prime hostelry, the Bear & Key, which, as shown later, derives from the town's sea-borne trading links with London. There are three signs which reflect the importance of the railway, but no sign bearing witness to that other widespread and lucrative operation - the 'free trade' of smuggling.

Other pubs were established in response to the growth of the town as houses sprang up along the winding main street and Victorian terraces expanded the town outwards. Whether they served the more affluent or the very poor, these were places where local people met together. A good draught of ale relieved the thirst during the hardships of a long and arduous working day, and in the evening a few more pints were needed over which to relax, perhaps with a game of skittles, or in mulling over the day's events, exchanging the latest gossip, recalling the personalities of the past and their adventures - and remembering disasters. For in the old town centre where pubs existed every few yards, even next to one another, they were inevitably caught up in the major crises of the town: the great fires and floods which have punctuated its history.

Until the mid-nineteenth century the larger inns were the only places with rooms large enough for people to meet together for organised entertainment, public meetings and for clubs and associations . When other public venues developed, this role faded, but the tradition of providing food as well as drink continued: the Annual Dinners and the special celebrations which recorded the fabric of local community life were still held in them.

In later years, as social standards changed and the old town was surrounded by estates of new houses, ancient inns were rebuilt, a few new ones were established and some faded from the scene. So the pubs have reflected the changing pattern and character of the town's population.

In this book text and illustration combine to explore this connection between the pubs and the gradual development of Whitstable and its character. The material is drawn essentially from printed sources, especially the pages of the Whitstable Times. This has tended to produce a bias towards the period before the First World War when the town was a much smaller place and and its everyday events were more newsworthy.

The book, then, might be called a pub crawl through the history of our town. As in the hostelries of earlier times, so here, there are some good stories well worth the telling.

A game of Skittles in the 'Snug'

1 THE ROAD TO CANTERBURY

Six hundred years ago, a well-worn track led seven miles inland from the Horsebridge. It went up along firm ground to the hamlet of Borstal, through the woodlands and heathland of Blean, then down to Canterbury.

Along this track, in fair weather and foul, trudged the fishwives of Whitstable. Fish was always wanted by the monks and priests and pilgrims of the cathedral city, so the weary way was worthwhile. We know the women walked the road as early as 1312 because it was then that Whitstable's Lord of the Manor claimed a patch of city land to be put aside for them: *'a certain liberty in the town of Canterbury...that all his tenants being fishermen shall have a certain place in the High Street between the Church of All Saints and the Church of Saint Andrew containing in length fourscore feet and in breadth three feet to sell their fish without giving toll to anyone...'.*

This important privilege was granted. Whitstable fish remained in demand, and in 1480 the fishwives moved to a special paved area in St. Margaret's Street, and later a market building was provided.

Then in 1523, John Roper, a leading landowner, saw room for further improvement to their lot, this time outside the city. In his will he bequeathed *'to the making of an horse way, for the fisshe wyves, and other, in the high way from Whitstaple, to the entring of the strete of Saincte Dunston, without the West Gate of Canterbury, in suche place, and places, as the Abbot of Faversham, that now is, and other myn executours, shall thinke most necessary and conveyent, one hundredth marks.'*

The need for 'an horseway' shows that by Tudor times not only fishwives, but pack horses and perhaps wheeled carts were making the journey. Two-way trade increased as the route to Canterbury up the Stour from Sandwich became silted. London, too, was developing and the use of Whitstable Bay was increasing. Till then, the settlement near the Horsebridge had probably been a mere scattering of cottages and huts, homes of fishermen, fishwives, and dredgermen. With prosperity, the number of sailors, pack-horse drivers and carters, thirsty men in need of good ale, grew apace. In 1593 John Colfe, a Canterbury brewer, was charged, *that he did sell to the people at Whitstable twenty barrels of beer called Bunner for eight shillings each which [price] exceeded that ordered by statute.'* The following year, Elias Martin was charged with overpricing 190 barrels. Men, overcharged or not, were not going thirsty. The first ale-houses may date from about this time, as a small village developed in what is now the western half of Harbour Street.

As shipping increased so the road towards Canterbury began to develop into today's straggling main street. The main exports to London were corn, hops, malt, and some cloth. Imports included coal from Northumberland and consumer goods for wealthy Canterbury; oranges and lemons, iron, brass, soap and cheese, all of them carried along that well-worn road.

The old Prince of Wales (earlier the Jolly Sailor) was probably known about this time under the sign of the Old Ship; deeds go back to 1626. It survived until 1898: a photograph shows a low timber building with heavy roof peg-tiles and large attic windows. In the dingy, low-beamed rooms many a smuggling plan may have been hatched, and many a preventive man hood-winked, as we describe in the next chapter. The inn's forecourt saw traditional activities up to Victorian times, when hucksters sold 'bargain prizes' and 'scanlins', peas fried in smelly fat which sold well especially to 'leaners and strollers'. Occasionally a more civilised Punch and Judy show turned up.

Another ale house later appeared nearby. In 1689 some 'undrained, very swampy and utterly unproductive land' was leased to Abraham Parren, a Canterbury inn-holder. He built a brick house, which became the Hoy Inn, and two cottages. His tenant, Edward Oliver of Whitstable, eventually bought the property and built a brick house which eventually became the Shades Inn, and this building survives to this day.

By the eighteenth century trade passing along that important road to Canterbury was continually increasing, especially as the Stour route to Canterbury through Fordwich became ever more silted. Daniel Defoe wrote in the 1720s; *'The citizens are obliged to fetch all their heavy goods, either from Fordwich, three miles off, or from Whitstable seven miles off; the latter they choose for such heavy goods as come from London; as oyl, wine grocery etc., because 'tis the less hazard by sea...'* By his time there were regular

6

Hoy, Prince of Wales & Shades
Lower High Street area

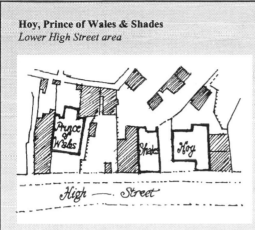

The Hoy, the Prince of Wales and the Shades - in Victorian times these three public houses were a notable feature of the Lower High Street, then called 'Cheapside'. They were situated within a few yards of each other, occupying a plot of charity land.

In 1698 the Trustees for the Poor leased half an acre to Abram Paren of Canterbury, and here he built a brick house which he let to Edward Oliver. In 1708 Oliver was able to buy the property from Paren's widow. He then built another brick house close by and moved into this. The original house became an inn, listed in 1730 as the Hoy, but it is likely that this was a change of name from the 'Old Ship' which ceases in that year ('Old' because there was a 'New Ship', which later became the Bear & Key). John Pilcher was landlord at this time. In 1791 the ownership passed to Thomas Foord, banker and landowner, and he carried out very necessary repairs to the weather-board extension which had been built to the street-line; the timber came from his estate at Chestfield. Around the 1820s the Canterbury brewers Rigden and Delmar leased the inn, and so also later did Shepherd Neame. By 1845 it was known as the Hoy Endeavour and this lasted until the 1860s. The old inn closed down at the end of 1906, and was later pulled down, making way for the towering block of Court's furniture showrooms.

The "new brick house" which Edward Oliver built still survives as Nos. 17 & 19 in the High Street. Nineteen became a public house quite late, being noted first in 1878. In 1903 it was stated to be "conducted as a small hotel" and "served the respectable class, sailors not allowed", it did not sell "four ale". The Shades, as it was called, specialised in dinner parties and its rather quiet character contrasted with its two neighbours. It closed at the end of 1906 also, under the Government's compensation scheme to reduce the enormous number of licensed premises.

The Prince of Wales, or the Jolly Sailor as it was earlier known, occupied a really old building which deeds trace back to 1626: a low, largely timbered building with a heavy peg-tile roof. Traditionally it was regarded as a ancient inn, but in fact as licensed premises it was a beerhouse dating after the Act of 1830 which permitted these to be set up. It is first named in 1851 with Thomas Adams as landlord, and he is also noted as 'Master Butcher'. It is however possible that the tradition is a recollection that there was an inn here much earlier. In 1723 there was an inn called the Hart, run by Mary Willard, and a lease for these premises in 1709 is in the name of one Richard Willard. The Hart disappears from the Justices records in 1731. So it could be to these years that the smuggling associations of the inn belong. In Victorian times the forecourt of the Jolly Sailor was a favourite gathering place for stalls and entertainments, the inn itself was noted for its quoits alley. Following the wedding of the Prince of Wales in 1863 the landlord Thomas Gann changed the name to celebrate the event and perhaps give the old inn a more up-to-date image. In 1898 the building was demolished by Flint & Sons and the new one was set up to the street-line. The Prince of Wales closed in 1967 and the building is today the Job Centre.

Prince of Wales

sailings of hoys between Whitstable and London. An advertisement of the time announced:

> **STEPHEN MATTHEW**
> Now intending to sail with his Hoy the Canterbury
> **From Whitstable to London this Saturday and every other Saturday**
> **As JOHN WELLS us'd to do..**
> **NB The HOY is fitted up with extraordinary Conveniences for**
> **Passengers.**

The road became over-used: it was *'in many parts thereof very narrow and... by reason of many heavy Carriages and great numbers of Passengers passing through the same, is in the Winter Season become ruinous and unsafe for Travellers and Carriages...'.* In 1736, its importance was recognised by Act of Parliament, and it was made a turn-pike, only the second in Kent, the first being the turn-piking of a stretch of the Dover Road.

More people were then able to travel the road by covered wagon (or 'carravan'), though not without problems, as an offer for two guineas reward offered for lost property illustrates: *'Lost out of Mr Hoclesh's carravan, going from Canterbury to Whitstable, a Sack, and in it a Silk gown and Petticoat, a trunk full of Head and other Linnen, eleven shillings in Money, a Pair of*

Royal Naval Reserve (Rose)
High Street

Originally a very narrow property, one of four in a block built by George Jennings of Canterbury around 1760, so beginning building development on the west side of the High Street. The old building still retains its peg-tile roof and the facade indicates four original tenements. Joseph Ballard owned the house from 1785 to 1843 and his last tenant Thomas Appleton may have established the beerhouse in the 1840s. Certainly the succeeding owner, John Giles, who bought it in 1843, is listed as a licensee. Much legal action followed his death in 1862 as his estate had to be divided between 45 nephews and nieces! The brewers Rigden & Delmar leased the beerhouse and it was enlarged by extending to the house next door. In 1876 the name was changed from the

1890

Rose to the Royal Naval Reserve: they used to practice gunnery at the battery down at Seasalter. In 1893 W.E. & J. Rigden purchased the pub. It is now a Whitbread's 'house'. The interior still retains much of the atmosphere of an old inn.

Scissars with a silver Chain, a black petticoat with two home-made Shirt Cloths in it, a flower'd Gown, and several other things...'. Someone's lady was not pleased...

This increase in commercial activity saw changes in the ale-houses and inns, some of the old 'houses' ended and new ones were established. The Old Ship went in 1730, but this very traditional sign of the Ship had already been taken by a new inn in 1703, which later changed to the Bear & Key. The Hart ended in 1731 while the Rose & Crown ran from 1729 to 1738. The Red Lion at the end of Harbour Street was established in 1733. The Duke of Cumberland, dating from 1748, was a continuation of the earlier Noah's Ark. Further along

Two Brewers
Canterbury Road

1671 George Vallence sold to Thomas Pott, a husbandman of 'Hearnhill' a cottage for £25. In 1692 Pott left his"House Backside and Barn" to his wife. The inn, the Two Brewers, was in existence in 1723; Thomas Wright was the inn-keeper. It occupied a significant site for here an ancient trackway came up from the shore, crossed the road and went away over Duncan Down, and in front of the inn the traditional Dredgermen's Fair was held until around 1850. 1731 the inn was leased by Thomas Tilbe, a brewer of St. Dunstan's in Canterbury. Later it was leased to John Cantis another local brewer, and then in 1785 it was sold to John Abbott of Thanet. The inn keeper at this time was May Sennock. 1825 Rest Flint (later Flint & Co) bought the Two Brewers. In 1858 Stephen Saddleton became licensee, he also owned the forge opposite and was a farmer. The most noticeable licensee was Arthur Betram who came in 1923 after 30 years as a theatre manager in London. Probably his retirement choice of Whitstable came through contact with the Irving family who lived at the Windmill on Borstal Hill. Bertram was a most flamboyant character full of acecdotes of theatre life; on Sundays he would announce opening time by playing on a set of bells which had once been a famous 'prop' used by Sir Henry Irving. He was 'mine host' well into his eighties.

the road in the early eighteenth century was the Packet Hoy, known even earlier as the 'Three Mariners', owned as we shall see by Thomas Reynolds who had connections with the smuggling trade.

Further into what was then the country, there was the Two Brewers inn; the present substantial brick building actually dates from that time. From its size it must have been an important hostelry. Opposite, on an open space called Greenstead or Grince Green one of Whitstable's three fairs - the Dredgerman's - was held annually on old St. James Day, August 4th. It's strange that the patron saint of oystermen should have been honoured so far from the waterfront (where there was an Easter fair), and perhaps the reason goes back a very long time indeed. For it was here that the way to Canterbury was crossed by another track which old records show came across the Salts from the seashore. Inland this pathway can be traced over Duncan Down to a ford on the Stour, bypassing Canterbury. It is possible that this track may be pre-Roman and even an ancient Iron Age salt-way.

Miss Elizabeth Pearson noted in her diary for August 5th 1797 that after visiting the vicarage she went to 'Trollop Fair', a clear indication that women of easy virtue were to be found there, and of course all sorts of things went on at country fairs. Half a century later non-conformist chapels were keeping the town's children away by giving them a treat, *'thus providing something in the way of a counter-attraction and keeping the children out of mischief.'* Tempting places, fairs.

The fair was still being held in the middle of the last century, in May: *'The annual fair was held on Thursday, and passed off in a very satisfactory manner, there being no disturbances of any importance. Cheap John, of course, was there selling off the usual services of crockery at the customary sacrifice, the supply of ginger-bread was large, and, we believe, fully equalled the consumption. Swings abounded, and "Har y'ar, forty in the middle", from the shooting galleries, sounded as a harmonious chorus down the street. The visitors to the town, chiefly from the neighbouring villages, seemed thoroughly to enjoy themselves, and their conduct, so far as we observed, was unexceptionable.'* Doubtless the Two Brewers did a roaring trade at what was a typical country fair which brought in people from the surrounding area. Local tradition has it that livestock was once sold, and a kind of 'circus' locally called a 'Horsemanship' held, but no details of this survive.

Gradually the event died, though folk memories die harder, for in later Victorian years the space was still occasionally being used: there is, for

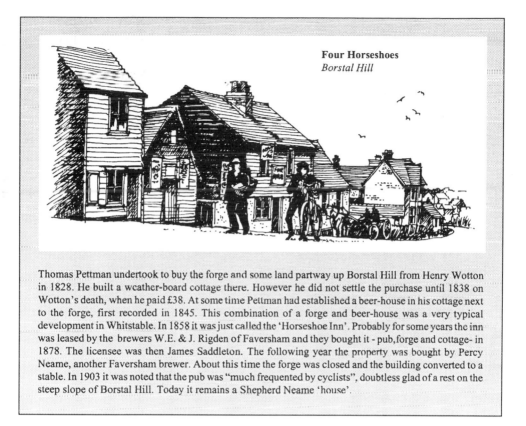

Four Horseshoes
Borstal Hill

Thomas Pettman undertook to buy the forge and some land partway up Borstal Hill from Henry Wotton in 1828. He built a weather-board cottage there. However he did not settle the purchase until 1838 on Wotton's death, when he paid £38. At some time Pettman had established a beer-house in his cottage next to the forge, first recorded in 1845. This combination of a forge and beer-house was a very typical development in Whitstable. In 1858 it was just called the 'Horseshoe Inn'. Probably for some years the inn was leased by the brewers W.E. & J. Rigden of Faversham and they bought it - pub, forge and cottage- in 1878. The licensee was then James Saddleton. The following year the property was bought by Percy Neame, another Faversham brewer. About this time the forge was closed and the building converted to a stable. In 1903 it was noted that the pub was "much frequented by cyclists", doubtless glad of a rest on the steep slope of Borstal Hill. Today it remains a Shepherd Neame 'house'.

example, a report in 1884 of hundreds of people watching a 100 yards race there, organised by the Running Club.

Further along the Toll Road, on the steep incline up Borstal Hill, two beer-houses developed, offering a rest for horses and men. The Four Horseshoes, as its name suggests, was established alongside a blacksmith's forge. In 1903 it was noted for more modern transport - the craze of cycling. Then on the brow of the hill was the Long Reach. Its name has a sea-faring ring but here refers to the long heavy pull needed to reach the top of nearby Clapham Hill. Its reputation in 1903 was not respectable, catering 'for poachers and the roughest class of people in Whitstable.'

In January 1884 an inquest was held in the Long Reach. To hold an inquest at an inn was not in itself unusual, but the events surrounding the death were so bizarre that the Whitstable Times office was besieged by a crowd anxious to read about it. Over 1,000 copies had to be printed immediately; the story even appeared in the London press.

From an early age, Fanny Wood had been a sickly child, the fruit of an illicit union. In adolescence she became subject to attacks of hysteria - a local doctor once mistakenly pronounced her dead, nearly causing a like fate for the parents who later in the night saw her move.

After another attack, kindly neighbours called, bringing gifts of food and money, whereupon Fanny confined herself to her bed for twenty years in a darkened room. Her face became mysteriously blackened except for a strange white mark down her nose. She was paralysed except for one arm, and could take only brandy and water and light dainties. She baffled three doctors; how she could eat was a mystery, she constantly vomited solid food; the parish allowed her half a bottle of restorative brandy a week. She became known for her perfect resignation and readiness for death.

When she was thirty-five, her brother was sentenced to six weeks' imprisonment for some slight offence. For some reason, this immediately restored Fanny to health. She sat up and wiped black charcoal from her face. Her mother, on entering the room, exclaimed *'Oh Fanny you are white!'* *'Am I mother?'* was the reply, *'I felt as if something gave me three taps on the head and a thrill passed through me.'*

She was in fact near death, and made a full confession to Mr Reeves who often visited her. *'She showed him as well as others that her arm which had been bent under her for years, was as whole as the other, and that her feet which had been altogether useless were fully at her service.'*

At the inquest Fanny's death was put down to 'consumption and disease of the lungs', and the coroner in summing up said that this had been the most extraordinary case he had met with in 64 years experience. Her mother did not impress him. *'He was bound to say that he did not believe a single syllable uttered by the mother of the girl. Indeed, no one could believe that the mother had known nothing of the deception'.* And he went on to say, *'it was impossible that she, having been living there for a period of 20 years, had told everything she knew to the jury'.* But nothing could be proved; all that was known for certain was that the family was poor, and the likelihood was that the temptation to deceive had been too much for her and her strange daughter. That, of course, was mere supposition, and she went unpunished by the court.

But local people saw to it that she did not escape scot-free. An item in the Kentish Gazette the following Autumn reported that *'The effigy of the mother*

Long Reach
84 Borstal Hill

In 1858 Stephen Saddleton closed his 'forge up the hill', as William Pettman of the Guinea wrote to his son in Australia, and moved down to the Two Brewers and the forge opposite. He noted that "the house is let as a beer-house". So this is how the Long Reach came into being, offering refreshment to those who had pulled up the 'Long Reach' to the top of Clapham Hill, on the road from Canterbury. Here in 1884 was held the Inquest on Fanny Hill, the 'Great Imposter', who faked illness for years to elicit sympathy and invalid comforts (including brandy!) from the local people. In 1903, owned by Gardner & Co., it was found to be dirty throughout, catering for "poachers and the roughest class of people in Whitstable". Nevertheless the Long Reach survived until 1935 when the owners, Mackesons of Hythe, transferred to their new Long Reach Tavern on the recently opened highway, the Thanet Way.

Long Reach Beefeater Inn,
(Long Reach Tavern)
Thanet Way

This roadhouse-style public house was opened in 1936 on the recently completed highway, the Thanet Way, replacing the old beerhouse on Borstal Hill. It was built by the brewers Mackesons of Hythe at a cost of nearly £5000. In the early days traffic and trade were poor and it was derided locally as a white elephant. It prospered during the war years with many troops stationed in the area, and then later as road traffic generally increased and especially with a flood of coach outings to Margate. In 1980 the building was extended and the interior completely remodelled in Tudor style to create the image of a Beefeater Inn.

of the ill-fated woman has been burnt in the presence of the individual herself, while at work in the hop-garden, and matters became so unpleasant that she did not return to work.'

It was a curious echo of a macabre happening a hundred years earlier...

2 SMUGGLING DAYS

Near the brow of Borstal Hill, the chained body of a young man swung from a gibbet, the wind ruffling his hair, his sightless eyes gazing down upon the town. He was young John Knight, hanged for murder in 1780 as a member of a smuggling gang, and brought from the county place of execution as a grim reminder to the men of Whitstable of the dangers of smuggling in the 'free trade'.

That shadowy trade of smuggling grew through the centuries because governments imposed duties on goods passing in and out of the country, and where such laws exist there are profits to be made in breaking them. In the Middle Ages, most smuggling was to do with wool and cloth, and we know little of how the men of Whitstable profited from this. However, there are more records by the eighteenth century, when the emphasis had shifted to coinage, spirits and tobacco, and in the nineteenth century when it was principally tobacco. As for the twentieth century........!

14

Smugglers preparing to land illicit cargo

All the small ports along the south and south-east coast trade easily and legally across the Channel, so it's no surprise to find that smuggling was a regular part of working life. Whitstable was certainly no exception. Certain flourishing inns on the coast now mark points long connected with the 'free trade'. The Blue Anchor, the Rose in Bloom and the Sportsman are all near to old landing places on the Seasalter coast, a coast that fronted an inhospitable and remote area of marsh, a few farms and cottages, all backed by the hidden depths of Blean Forest.

This area, and indeed Whitstable as a whole, seemed to attract the attention of certain enigmatic people, men who led double lives. As local historian Wallace Harvey asks, *'What was there in such a desolate and lonely district to attract and hold the interest of successive generations of important people who lived in such distant places as Ashford and Dover? Why should people, who were ostensibly strangers to the locality, want to invest their money in property there? What was there about this particular district, at that*

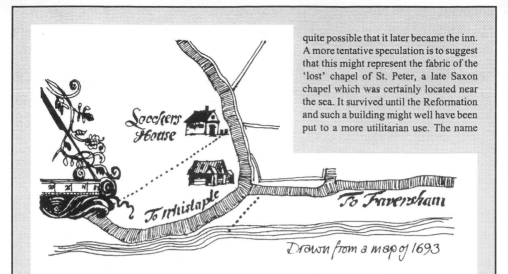

quite possible that it later became the inn. A more tentative speculation is to suggest that this might represent the fabric of the 'lost' chapel of St. Peter, a late Saxon chapel which was certainly located near the sea. It survived until the Reformation and such a building might well have been put to a more utilitarian use. The name

Drawn from a map of 1693

Blue Anchor (Crown, Rose & Crown)
Faversham Road, Seasalter

The Blue Anchor is one of the ancient inns of the area. It began as the Crown in 1744, became the Rose & Crown in 1751, then the Anchor in 1755, and finally settled in the next year as the Blue Anchor. This seems to have been a popular inn sign of the time; there were several locally. From the beginning until some time after 1770 the inn-keeper was John Codham. He therefore knew well the eccentric vicar of Seasalter at that time, the Rev Thomas Patten, of whom many tales are told. He openly kept a mistress, usually appeared dirty and unkempt, drove to church in an ox waggon, and was known to break off his sermon to go off merrily with willing members of the congregation to the Blue Anchor. The Archbishop complained, but he seems to have been popular with his flock. He was certainly happy to turn a blind eye to local smuggling activities. Indeed these often centred on the Blue Anchor itself, it is said. The first owner of the Blue Anchor was George Giles; it then passed to his grandson Giles Morgan who sold to John Rigden, brewer of Faversham in 1811 for £497.

The inn occupies a site very close to the location of the 'Lookers House' drawn on a map of 1693. The 'Looker' tended the livestock grazing on the marshes. This house appears quite substantial, surprisingly so for a shepherd's cottage. It is

Blue Anchor in ancient times was used as an ecclesiastical emblem. It indicates that it was the anchor of faith which kept Christians from being swept away by the storms of life. It seems possible that the name may have been chosen to link the Saxon chapel with the pub. It is interesting that the sketch map of 1693 depicts what might be two gravestones standing up beside the front of the building. The land area was later known as Vicarage Field; a piece of charity land.

Unfortunately there is no record of the appearance of the old Blue Anchor. The inn was rebuilt probably around 1900 and has been extended since. Ownership passed from W. E. & J. Rigden through brewery amalgamation to being a Whitbread's 'house' today.

particular period, that would induce people in a good station in life to seek and to obtain obscure and poorly paid positions in the customs service?'

The answer to these questions is a simple one. There were fortunes to be made master-minding the efforts of local lawbreakers.

One of the most imposing houses ever built in Whitstable was Oxford House, on the site now occupied by the Library. Its builder and first owner, Mr. Thomas King, had at one time been Customs Waiter and Searcher at Seasalter, and Tide Surveyor at Whitstable, and would thus have appeared to be strictly on the side of the law. But he seems to have made a fortune quite at odds with his salary and was able to retire to Dover by all accounts a sleek and respectable citizen. His son Jonas also held the post of Coastal Waiter at Whitstable, and it was he who lived in the grand house. That there was something hidden in his life, however, is indicated when he was forced to advertise a reward of 50 guineas in 1801, *' for the conviction of those who frequently broke the windows of Mr. King the Revenue Officer of Whitstable in the middle of the night'.* Did he favour some and not others? Not surprisingly, he moved and sold the house in 1804.

The purchaser was a Mr. Baldock, another gentleman who had risen from humble origins by mysterious means. In early life he had been *'a poor boy employed to look after cows, and remarkable for dirtiness and slovenliness.'* But somehow he did well, and worked up many connections with local farms and properties. One of them was Seasalter Farm, situated opposite the Rose in Bloom. This inn was close to the Old Haven landing place, one of those that made Seasalter marshes so attractive to wealthy gentlemen of humble origins and dubious practices.

Baldock is believed to have developed a safe route for contraband goods through to Canterbury. He built two houses in the Turnpike Road, and these, it is said, together with several other farms and cottages, formed part of a linked signalling system right down into Whitstable. Warning of any movement by the Revenue or Dragoons by day was indicated by raising a besom on a long pole out of a chimney or tree-top. At night signalling was done by raising and lowering a lantern at a window. In town the news was spread by simple unspoken messages: pulling the nose meant danger; stroking the chin implied 'alert' - a cargo was on the move. When Baldock died he was said to be *'possessed of one million and one hundred thousand pounds'.* By that time he had gone heavily into property, building Canterbury Barracks and leasing them to the government at the rate of 6d a week for each soldier. Nevertheless

17

Rose in Bloom
Joy Lane

The original building was an old weather-board thatched cottage which stood near the pathway which led up from the beach on to Scab's Acre and then crossed the road to Seasalter Farm opposite. The beginning of this old route can be seen on the right hand side of Turner's famous view of Whitstable (Scab's Acre was largely destroyed by the railway cutting). This was a much used smuggler's landing point and probably the cottage on the road played a part as a look-out point. The beer-house is first noted here in 1861 when Stephen Hunt was landlord. This was quite an isolated position then, so trade must have come from farm workers, travellers and naval men practising down at the Battery. In 1898 Mackeson's the brewers of Hythe purchased the pub and in a couple of years built the present

Rose in Bloom. This was doubtless in anticipation of the estate development off Joy Lane, which in fact did not really take off until the 1930s. The old building was restored and enlarged to become a house called 'Treetops'. Some years ago this was pulled down to make room for the larger car-park. The Rose in Bloom is a Whitbread's 'house'.

his obituary did add discreetly that he *'continued to acquire wealth in various ways'.*

The connection between the sudden wealth of such men and the preventive service was surely too much of a coincidence.

Smuggling is by its very nature secret and clandestine. These rich magnates of smuggling relied on the illegal activities of hundreds of lesser men, and it is only in the dry details of court proceedings, old newspaper cuttings and in half-believed, whispered anecdotes that a picture of it begins to emerge from the shadows. As late as 1870 the obituary notice of an old Seasalter man recorded: *'when young he followed the then respectable calling of a smuggler as he was fond of telling us, at a time when, in his own words, "he smuggled, the parish clerk was a smuggler, and he wasn't sure the parson didn't."'*

It is true that some men of the cloth were not above augmenting their stipends in this way. It was certainly true of the eccentric Rev. Thomas Patten, as this 1746 report shows; *'Dear Sir, I beg to acquaint you that on the 7th instant a gang of about one hundred and fifty smugglers landed their cargo between Reculver and Birchington and went from the sea coast about 9.0 a.m. Sixty three men and eighty to ninety horse went by Whitstable and Faversham, and the rest over Grove Ferry. The Rev Thomas Patten of Whitstable has let*

18

*the Commisioners know when some gangs went through Whitstable for
Faversham. It is reported that the Doctor formerly received tithe from some
of the smugglers, but these gangs, being such rugged colts (as the Doctor calls
them), that nothing is to be got by them, made him angry.'*

The extract clearly shows the extent of the business at that time, and makes
it clear that by then the smuggling operations, with their network of hide-
aways and signal stations, had developed into a highly organised business.
Whitstable was as advanced as any, perhaps even more so than some. The
historian Hasted reported that Whitstable smugglers had developed a specialised lantern for signalling from ship to shore. Its main feature was a long
tapering funnel about six feet long which made the light visible without
radiation when directed at the spot where receivers were known to be waiting
on shore. Much thought and ingenuity were being applied at all levels and the
business was becoming more elaborate.

By the mid-eighteenth century organised gangs had developed, the members of which were not afraid to use violence, particularly as the Revenue
Service failed to match their growth. Preventive officers still patrolled singly
or in groups that were too small to cope with the large and growing gangs.
Indeed, since they couldn't beat them, they all too often joined them, accepting
pay and handouts in return for turning a blind eye.

As late as 1825 there is a record of a revenue man being bribed to do just
that. John Hudson of Whitstable was fined £100 for 'being concerned in a
smuggling transaction.' One of the witnesses against Hudson, a revenue
officer called George Lawson, had received gifts from him and had been
encouraged to do so by his superiors, becoming therefore a double agent. On
the night in question, *'Hudson, with about 14 other persons came down to the
beach [at Swalecliffe], where Lawson was stationed, and gave him some
spirits. Hudson and his party then hauled a boat ashore, and took out 15 half-
ankers, upon which Lawson seized Hudson with two tubs on his back, and fired
his pistol as a signal, and he was
captured.'*

The appearance of large gangs
led inevitably to the employment of
the military, and pitched battles and
lesser skirmishes were not unknown.
It was on 26th February 1780 that
the 'Battle of Borstal Hill' was joined.

A large smuggling lugger was

Smuggler's signalling Lantern.

19

driven ashore at Whitstable. 183 tubs of Spirits were aboard, a valuable prize, and Joseph Nicholson, Supervisor of Excise, enlisted the aid of the military to move it under guard from the district. A corporal and eight troupers of the Fourth Dragoons got to the ship and unloaded her, probably before the very eyes of the smugglers. Nicholson had decided to make for Canterbury with the captured contraband, even though it meant that they would have to go up the steep Toll Road that climbed Borstal Hill, a deeply cut way overhung by trees and shrubs; perfect for an ambush.

The heavily laden wagon began the slow ascent, and then, as they reached the steepest part of the hill, a shout from the smugglers demanded they gave up the spirits. Before they had a chance to respond, a burst of firing from the darkness rang out, followed by an attack by more than fifty smugglers, some from the lugger, and some from the district. In the fierce hand-to-hand mêlée that followed, two dragoons were killed and others injured. The soldiers were forced to flee, and the smugglers unloaded the wagon and vanished with all but two tubs of the precious Geneva into the darkness. They took their haul back to the lugger and its crew sailed away with it, leaving the Whitstable men to lie low.

A reward of fifty guineas and a free pardon was announced, and within a couple of weeks John Knight of Whitstable had been betrayed. He was charged on the 12th March with 'aiding and assisting in the murder of two dragoons at Whitstable in this County.' At the assizes in Maidstone, he was swiftly found guilty. *'It appeared by the evidence on the trial that he was one of the men who fired a signal gun to assemble the smugglers, and that he was afterwards seen to load his piece with a leaden bullet, and that he among others actually fired when two of the dragoons were shot. He had no defence to make, but said he had only fired once in the air, and seemed utterly insensible of the nature of his crime.'*

Within a few days he was hanged on Penenden Heath near Maidstone, the county's traditional site of executions. *'His behaviour at the place of execution, was such as became his unhappy situation, and just before he was turned off, begged of the spectators to take warning how they assist smugglers. He said he was at that time ignorant of the nature of the crime he had committed, and was drawn in by the persuasions of those who knew better... He died very penitent, and the people seemed to be greatly affected at seeing a young man cut off in the flower of his youth. He was not 18 years old.'* As was customary, his corpse was brought from Maidstone and displayed on that gibbet on Borstal Hill as a warning to others.

Beaching the contraband.

He was convicted on the evidence of 'Edward Edenden and others of Whitstable'. Fifty guineas was a large sum for those days, but the revenge on informers by the smugglers could be savage indeed. Why then did these local men take the risk? Perhaps there was rivalry between local smuggling gangs, and poor John Knight was an unfortunate victim.

Nevertheless Edenden did not get off entirely scot-free. Tradition has it that he was punished for his 'crime' in a most macabre fashion. On its first night on the gibbet some person or persons unknown took down the corpse and disappeared with it into the night. Next morning, when he opened his door, Ted Edenden found, tied to the knocker, its sightless eyes upon him, the chained body of young John Knight. Even then, he was luckier than one Uden who was tarred and feathered, then dragged up and down the ditches till he was exhausted; the report says that 'he did not last long after this.' A final twist to that tale is that the old recollections remark that Uden was actually innocent. Somehow he had been caught up in the complicated web of crime and counter crime, in which men on the fringes of the market in contraband goods acted to their best advantage as day followed day and fortunes swayed.

And Knight's death had little effect. Within a few months it was reported that the gang who had murdered the two dragoons had captured a loaded collier and taken the ship to France, so adding piracy to their list of crimes.

Not all smuggling was carried out by big gangs, however; it was a lucrative sideline for local fishermen and oyster dredgers. The French, indeed, encouraged them; an export house in Cherbourg that supplied 200 gallons of brandy a month expressly for sale to smugglers was a not unusual feature of

21

Brewery Tap
20 Oxford Street

First noted as a beerhouse in 1856, licensee George Iggulden; possibly recorded 1858 as the Coach & Horses beershop. Developed as an outlet for the Whitstable brewery (located opposite today's Library). It was purchased from the Daniels family in 1866 by Johnson & Co of Canterbury. The small bar was built out from an ancient cottage, which partly remains at the rear, and which had strong smuggling association, with a tunnel, it is said, going under the road to Ivy House opposite. Closed due to limited trade in 1911. Then it became part of Fred Breach's garage, the first in the town, and here he generated the first electricity which supplied the 'picture house' next door. Today the building is an Indian Restaurant.

French ports.

The final decades of the eighteenth century thus saw smuggling at its height, and the local papers had regular reports of seizures by the authorities. In the year 1788-9 no fewer than thirteen such seizures were made that concerned Whitstable: *'Thursday night was taken at Tankerton a smuggling boat with 120 casks of foreign spirits... Friday night was taken near Whitstable, a smuggling yawl belonging to Essex with foreign spirits aboard... Thursday morning was seized at Whitstable by two excise officers, thirteen casks of foreign spirits...Thursday afternoon was taken by Dover excise Cutter, a large smuggling yawl, belonging to Whitstable...'* and so on.

Sometimes, inevitably, local boats were intercepted, searched and contraband found, but, if time allowed, the tubs of spirits would hastily be thrown overboard, roped together so as to be recovered later. But there were risks, as in a somewhat garbled newspaper account of Tuesday , March 29th, when: *'One day last week a boat with four men, belonging to Whitstable, endeavouring to fish up some tubs of liquor which had been thrown overboard off Reculver point, till the opportunity offered for running them on shore, by a sudden wave, while the men were hauling in the rope, was overset, two of them, by clinging to the oars and tubs were taken up by a vessel near at hand, but the other two, notwithstanding they were good swimmers, were unfortunately drowned.'*

Smuggling activities were not by any means confined to the lonely windswept shores of Seasalter or the clay cliffs of Tankerton and Swalecliffe.

Whitstable town itself was certainly heavily involved in the 'free trade'. Take Ozias Kemp, a respectable man with a tobacconist's shop in Harbour Street. He had a beach boat-house nearby on Sea wall and here he would sit betimes of an evening a-reading his bible by the light of a candle. The showing of its flame was an indication to the smugglers that the Excise men were abroad and they should not attempt to land their cargo of tobacco. When it was decided safe, the flame would be put out. Ozias received a cut from the contraband, of course, and so, no doubt, did some of his regular customers.

Much of such smuggling was carried on, so tradition tells us, near to Ozias, around the landing point on the Horsebridge right in the centre of Old Whitstable. The illegal goods were probably brought ashore in the false bottoms of the carts that brought in legal loads of coal.

Once landed, contraband had to be hidden from the Revenue Officers. The story is told of the Jolly Sailor Inn (later the Prince of Wales) that once when a cargo of tobacco had been brought in the word came that the Excise men were on their way down Borstal Hill. Lacking a suitable hiding place, the local men quickly formed a line across the road to a house that was being built opposite. The parcels were passed from hand to hand and stacked under a large tarpaulin. When the Revenue Officers arrived there were just two old men having a quiet drink in the deserted bar. Across an equally deserted street many unseen eyes were enjoying the frustration of the searching officers.

As in all towns with smuggling associations, Whitstable is not short of tales of secret rooms and underground passages. Many of these probably belong to local folk-lore, but there are eye-witness accounts of some such features at the old Brewery Tap public house. This fronted a much more ancient building which backed on to the open Salts, and thus had direct access to the sea. Here a hiding place has been described and also a tunnel which went under the road to the old Ivy House which stood opposite, in which there was concealed shelving behind false panelling.

Yet another ancient inn with smuggling associations was the Packet Hoy, earlier known as the 'Three Marriners'. It belonged to the Reynolds family, and in the early eighteenth century Thomas Reynolds was said to have been the organising genius behind a large smuggling gang. He, like William Baldock nearly a century later, owned a series of properties across the countryside behind Whitstable, which would have eased the passage by pack horse of illicit goods towards Lenham and the main smuggling route to London. Locally, two farms were used in an emergency: Seasalter Cross, where it was said, haystacks could double in size overnight, and Pink Farm which had a number of hiding places: *'On either side of the great open fireplace was a large cupboard lined with shelves. The back of the cupboard on the right-hand side was actually a door disguised by its shelves. When the house was demolished about 1953, this door was found to give access to a secret room about ten feet square... The centre bedroom, which was next to the great chimney, had no windows. In the dark corner behind the chimney was a kind of shaft about two feet square, with iron rungs across one corner. This shaft led down to the secret room... The shaft provided an ideal means of passing food and drink down to anyone hiding there, or indeed a way of escape if the room was unfortunately discovered.'*

But not all the illicit goods left Whitstable. *'On Tuesday was seized by three Excise officers and a party of dragoons, ten casks and four stone bottles of foreign spirits, from persons who sell without licenses, at Whitstaple.'* And, as described in a local account, *'In this way there was much drunkenness and fighting, there were little shops called pop shops where one could get his liqour on the cheap.'*

Smugglers did not care overmuch for the aims of their government in other matters than the import of dutiable goods. During the war years from 1793 to 1814 Whitstable smugglers were involved in the more unusual movement of human cargo: they helped French prisoners of war to escape back to France. Captured French officers were allowed to live out on parole in certain towns, and if enough in the way of bribes was forthcoming from their relatives in France, then passage could be arranged, probably in disguise, to a suitable boat, perhaps at Whitstable. But ordinary French prisoners were not so well treated, though whatever hardship their escape entailed was certainly less than

Fan
66 Herne Bay Road

No information has been found on this inn. It was a weather-board building next to this cottage and is believed to have played a part in the scheme whereby French prisoners of war were smuggled back to France during the Napoleonic era.

the fearful and degrading treatment they received in the notorious prison hulks of the Thames and Medway. These worn-out rotting ships housed, in overcrowded, insanitary and disease-ridden conditions, thousands of prisoners captured in war. Desperate, some escaped. Most such unfortunates embarked sick and in filthy rags or even naked on one of the many hoys which sailed watchfully up and down the Thames, before being landed near to the

Packet Hoy (Three Marriners)
1-3 Oxford Street

This early inn appears as the forerunner of the rather grand Georgian house which lies behind the shopfronts here. The licensing records show an inn noted as "Now the Canterbury Hoy" ending in 1729. Deeds indicate that it was earlier the "Three Marriners". The inn was owned and possibly occupied by Thomas Reynolds who had a great reputation for running a smuggling gang in the early eighteenth century.

Blue Anchor Inn. From here, regardless of their condition, they would be hustled up to Pye Alley Farm on the Turnpike Road and there given life-saving food and decent clothing. Then, by devious lanes and across country they would reach and hide in Convicts Wood, supplied with food from Brooklands Farm. When all was arranged, including no doubt the payment of 'ransom money', the group would move as swiftly as their condition allowed along the stream to the then-remote area of Swalecliffe. There they would go down to Long Rock, where their boat was waiting, and climb aboard for France. Here, too, the enterprise is remembered in the old name of Convicts Bay.

Although no written records of this route are to be found, local tradition,

Jolly Sailor
Faversham Road, Seasalter

1730, a deed records a field of just over an acre here, part of a farm at "Bostal-Green" owned by Capt. Richard Clement. This was purchased by William Court in 1809 and here he built a cottage and stable. Probably in the 1830s Court established a beerhouse. Although the location was then very isolated, close by on the shore was the Coastguard Station. And for travellers between Whitstable and Seasalter there was a necessary and perhaps welcome break here, for outside on

the road was the 'Clapp Gate': a swing gate positioned to contain the livestock grazing along the coastal marsh. Ownership of the beershop and land passed to Francis Seamen and then A.D. Curling. In 1898 it became one of the many local pubs owned by Flint & Co of Canterbury. They extended the old building and it was known for some years as the Jolly Sailor Hotel. More recently it has been extensively modernised both inside and out; it is now a Whitbread's 'house'.

repeated down the years, has doubt-less passed on the details of this unusual aspect of Whitstable's smuggling story. Like much of that story, it was carried on under the noses of the authorities. For it was during the Napoleonic War that the Government established a coastal blockade manned by the Royal Navy; there were stations at Seasalter, Fish House (?), Whitsta-

Pye Alley Farm

ble, Tankerton, and, yes, at Swalecliffe.

Contraband goods which were successfully confiscated locally were taken to the Watch House at Whitstable. Traces of this massive lock-up store were discovered in 1949 during rebuilding work which was being carried out in Reeves Alley. Part of its foundation wall, three feet thick, was uncovered.

Even small quantities of captured goods, however, still put Revenue Officers at risk. In May 1825, Mr. Edward Hunt, Comptroller and Coastwaiter at Whitstable, seized 23 tubs of contraband spirits, and put them for safe keeping into the Whitstable Watch House. The liquor might have been safe, but as for poor Mr. Hunt... *'Whilst proceeding in a cart on the road to Faversham, a number of men, with their faces blacked, and with sticks in their hands, leaped over a hedge, dragged the said Edward Hunt out of the cart and threw him into a hedge with his face downwards, and otherwise violently assaulted him.'*

Nevertheless the efforts of the government began to bear fruit, and by the middle of the nineteenth century, smuggling had been much reduced - or at any rate driven underground. However, fears that the introduction in 1831 of the new-fangled coastguard system would seriously interfere with what remained of the free trade were ill-founded. In Seasalter, the real home of local smuggling, one Edward Gaskin would act as a decoy when a landing was planned, and he would lead the Coastguards a merry dance away across the marshes. And, as if by magic, a barrel of brandy or a supply of tobacco would be found near the Coastguard station the next morning.

Old habits take a long time a-dying, and in dealing with local smuggling, we are in fact deep in the world of coincidence and hints and knowing looks. *'Smuggling, why it was not known or even dreamt of or breathed of. Had you* spoken to any of these worthies about it, they would have raised their hands with a heavenly gesture, and with a look of innocence on their faces, told you it was a sin to be shunned like the plague (particularly if there was the slightest suspicion). But what a tale was unfolded when these cronies met in the snuggery of old Jack's store! The chuckles and smothered laughter that was heard occasionally, the gurgle, gurgle (was it water?) leaving the mouth of the demi-john and finding its way into a cup or glass, the peculiar taste of Holland's the crew found when drinking out of the tea-pot later on. The blame was put on the kettle, and yet it was supposedly empty when they left the shore. The small kegs of... (I don't believe it was water somehow) decently interred in the beach, their exhumation and post mortem performed on them later, with glass and cup or any receptacle that would not leak; other casks sunk and marked for the time being in the dykes of the marshes at Seasalter.'

While we may gently smile at such recollections, we would do well to remember the grim price paid by such as John Knight and innocent Mr. Uden.

Preventitive Officers
giving chase

3 FISHERMEN & DREDGERS

'I remember being sometimes awakened early on a winter's morning by the Company's bellman. Then I could hear my grandfather stirring, and later I could hear doors in Sydenham Street shutting, and the tramp, tramp of seaboots (heavy leather boots reaching nearly to the thigh) of the dredgermen going to their storehouses and boats. As a boy, I liked being on the beach watching the dredgermen going to their storehouses, bringing out their oars and tackle, launching their skiffs, and rowing out to their yawls. Then the sails of the yawls would be set, and casting off from their moorings, the boats would sail to their appointed task, towing their skiff behind.'

So one old salt remembers a scene from his boyhood at the turn of the century as Whitstable carried on its ancient lawful industry.

Anyone who has heard of Whitstable, will say, 'Ah, yes, Oysters.'

28

Old Harbour and Fishermen's Stores 1885

The Thames estuary has been noted for oysters since Roman times, and Whitstable in particular has long been famous for them. In the time of Dickens, Whitstable was exporting about 124 million oysters a year to London, where they formed a cheap and highly nutritious diet for ordinary people. As journalist John Hollingshead wrote in 1859, *'Many important towns, in many parts of England exist upon one idea: and Whitstable, though not very important, is amongst the number. Its one idea is Oysters. Its aspect is not sightly if looked at with an eye that delights in the stuccoed terraces and trim gravelled walks of a regular watering place; for the line of its flat coast (which*

29

takes up one side of a bay formed by the Swale, a branch of the Medway) is occupied by squat wooden houses, made soot-black with pitch, the dwellers in which are sturdy freeholders, incorporated free-fishers, or oyster dredgers, joined together by the ties of a common birthplace, by blood, by marriage, and trade.'

For long, the men of the oyster industry dominated Whitstable. At its height they had about eighty fishing-smacks and fourteen market hoys in their fleet. On three days of each week, in fair weather and foul, the crews of the fishing boats were busy out on the oyster-beds, taking samples, testing specimens, sifting out and killing enemies of the oyster such as the poisonous star-fish, and transferring young oysters to places where they would find the most nourishment. On the other three days of the week, they dredged mature oysters for the rich London market. Then the hoys were able to sail to Billingsgate, and the dredgermen could return to their warm and glowing firesides inside wooden houses 'soot-black with pitch'.

On the night of Monday 8th October 1866 the inevitable happened, as it had happened before. A great fire swept through that soot-black jumble of fishermen's stores, sail-lofts and workshops, all of tarred weatherboarding. It engulfed and destroyed not only many oyster-dredgers huts, but two of its ancient inns: The Red Lion and the Duke of Cumberland. Close by, the other major hostelry of the town, The Bear & Key, happily escaped.

These three inns had grown up next to one another. This area, known as The Cross, together with the Horsebridge, had long formed a focus for local trade, and it was around them that the town had grown. Near here oysters, fish, and that important commodity coal were landed, and from here, as described in Chapter 1 a road ran to Canterbury, six or seven miles away through the Forest of Blean.

There was little competition between the three establishments, because they each seem to have served different sections of the community. The Bear & Key, quite early on, became the most prestigious establishment and by the mid-nineteenth century, by then rightly called a hotel, was catering particularly for travellers. So central has it been to much of Whitstable's history that it has warranted a later chapter entirely to itself. The Red Lion, which did not rise from the ashes of the fire, seems to have been a centre for much of the town's social life outside the oyster industry, which we describe below.

It was for the oystermen that the third inn, The Duke of Cumberland, played a unique role. *'The free dredger is thoroughly independent, not given to touch his hat to lord or squire; and if he does pay any mark of respect to*

Side elevation

Duke of Cumberland (Noah's Ark)
The Cross, High Street

The inn, by the sign of the Duke of Cumberland, first appeared in 1748. This was a change of name from the Noah's Ark which probably goes back into the seventeenth century. Doubtless the Duke, second son of George II, was highly popular at the time, having in 1746 crushed the Scottish rebellion at Culloden. The landlord Robert Chandler changed the name the next year to the Duke William, which continued until 1758. An early origin for the inn is very likely considering its strategic position at the Cross - the meeting of the ways. In 1866 fire swept through the block containing the Duke and the Red Lion behind, so there is no knowledge of its appearance. Until then the inn had been the headquarters of the oyster dredgermen. Here they were paid out at the end of the day for their working 'stint', and in the large room upstairs the Annual Water Court was held. The Duke was rebuilt by the brewers Rigden & Delmar, and in 1878 as W.E. & J. Rigden they sold it to Neames also of Faversham for £100. This low figure suggests that the inn then was not large; included in the sale was a coalyard at the rear. It was probably extended to make the 'family and commercial hotel' which flourished under Mr

William Gurr in the 80s and 90s. During 1900-01 at a cost of over £4000 the Duke was modernised throughout and extended at the rear with a splendid billiard room, stables and a coach house. It had now replaced its rival opposite, the Bear & Key, as the town's premier establishment. But it, too, has declined from its heyday as the character of the central town area has changed. The Duke of Cumberland remains a Shepherd Neame 'house'; there has been an inn on this site for some 300 years or more.

the Duke of Cumberland it is only as the sign of the dredgers' public house, where the profits of the free company of oyster fishers are divided and paid.' Until the fire it was here that the freemen met at the end of each day to receive their pay-out from the day's dredging. If they had thought about it, they would probably have regarded themselves, not without justice, as the aristocracy of the town, important citizens upon whom the prosperity of all the rest of its citizens depended.

The daily share-out was routine: a bigger event happened at the Duke of Cumberland in July, when by tradition the second Thursday was Water Court Day. This, for Oystermen, was the highlight of the year, and naturally a gala day of celebration in the town. The oystermen put on clean white jerseys, and the town was decorated with flags and bunting. From the early hours of the morning men

---

Dredgerman's Arms
Sea Wall (now the yard of the Oyster Stores)

1853 William Philpott purchased ground here fronting the Sea Wall from the Commissioners of Sewers who owned the land along the wall. Here he built a cottage with two tenements, and in the right-hand one a beerhouse was opened. With its position next to the headquarters of the oystermen the name was doubtless intended to draw trade.
The license in 1858 was held by William Foreman and in 1862 by Philpott himself. 1885 Philpott sold the pub and the adjoining cottage to Frederick Flint for £500. 1903 the pub was found to be dirty with little business, being dependent on sailors - "the roughest class" - and it was closed. The property was then purchased by the Oyster Company for £250 and was pulled down to make additional space for the Oyster Stores building.

---

staggered along with immense boughs of decorative green bush and shrubs, while others strung bunting across windows of the 'Duke'. Then the festivities could begin, with up to 100 men hotly and convivially packed into an upper room.

'At ten o'clock a.m. the chairman took his seat with the foreman, treasurer and jury in close contact, the water bailiff standing close by their side, supporting a 6 feet oar, richly emblazoned with gold, as a staff to show the dignity of the company as well as himself. The chairman gave a dozen blows on the table with a substantial mallet, and the water bailiff as many thumps on the floor with his staff, and shouted "Silence, order," etc., which had the desired effect, for nearly half the persons present could hear the Chairman read over the orders of the

court, threatening to fine persons for non-attendance, presenting themselves intoxicated, or breaking down beacons, etc., etc. This part of the business having been finished without stopping more than ten times to call order, and all being so well satisfied, a general shout (amidst the ordinary hubbub) of "dinner, dinner, dinner time" came echoing from all parts of the room, to which the chairman assented by a nod.'

The menu was by custom, on those hot July days, wing ribs of beef or lamb and green peas, cherry and currant pie, and cheese, all accompanied by copious draughts of beer.

Red Lion
on the site 31-32 Harbour Street

The Red Lion was one of the three major Whitstable inns, located within a few yards of each other (the Duke of Cumberland and the Bear & Key remain today). It stood next to the rear of the Duke of Cumberland. The Red Lion was first licensed in 1733. It was totally destroyed by fire in 1866 which began in an adjacent carpenter's shop; this consumed the Duke as well. Although apparently fully insured the brewers Shepherd Neame did not rebuild it. This was surprising, for newspaper items for its later years reveal a flourishing establishment where 50 could sit down to an excellent dinner; it was home to the Foresters, the cricket club 'Whitstable United' and the Running Club. And here Whitstable and Herne Bay engaged in friendly rivalry at billiards.

After dinner, the election of officers and other business noisily proceeded until the final ritual, when *'the treasurer dealt out ten shillings a man for their devoted attention to the business of the day, and all took their departure with jollification, hearty good-will, and general satisfaction, knowing as they do that the stock on their grounds is worth over two hundred thousand pounds. "Hurrah! Hurrah!"*

But, whatever the dredgermen might have thought, life was not oysters, oysters and yet more oysters. The town was growing apace, and next door to the Duke there had been, until the great fire, the Red Lion, a tavern that catered for other groups and activities that were newly emerging. Newspaper reports record a number of societies and organisations meeting there regularly. The great Victorian Friendly Society, the Order of Foresters, met there from 1845, and doubtless their celebratory dinner was typical of many. *'An excellent dinner was provided by the worthy host to which about 40 sat down. After the cloth was cleared, the toasts and song went merrily round and many excellent addresses were delivered by the members of the order. The party broke up shortly after 12 o'clock, quite delighted with the pleasant evening they had spent together in the first Forester's Court in the town and port of Whitstable.'* The Foresters had still been using The Red Lion twenty years later. The Whitstable Running Club, whose members ran on The Salts (now the golf course), had their business and social meetings here, as did the Cricket Club, whose name, Whitstable United, is to us more typical of a football team. The fire of 1866 thus left a gap, for it had been a busy tavern.

The fire accelerated change in a time of change. As a spacious Music Hall had been built nearby, many of the societies gravitated there. Even though the Duke of Cumberland was rebuilt, the dredgermen broke with their ancient tradition and moved the Water Court to the new premises (though they had the lunch prepared as before in the Duke's kitchen),. It was truly the end of an era, now that there was this new public venue shortly to be renamed the Assembly Rooms. Gradually the role of licensed premises as centres of public and social events began to change. The Red Lion was not long missed. Whitstable was becoming a town.

By the end of the century the hallowed organisation of the oyster industry had also been forced into change. From 1898 the Freeman system was swept away and replaced by a modern share-holding Company. The Water Court no longer met. But as a reminder of earlier time there remains the Royal Native Oyster Stores building, dominating the Horsebridge as once the oyster industry had dominated the whole town.

'Foxy' Humphrey -
Dredgerman.

F76 'Gamecock'
Whitstable
Oyster 'Yawl'

4 SAIL & STEAM

Late in the 1820s the talk in the taverns of Whitstable Street, as the town was then called, was about the building of a 'Rail Road'. Many men were thirsty from digging cuttings, building embankments or excavating by candle-light a tunnel at Tyler Hill. It was through this that the iron trackway was planned to run from the Whitstable waterfront to the City of Canterbury.

The idea was not new to them. Whitstable had long had connections through the coal trade with the industrial north. Up there tramways were well established, and in 1825 Stephenson had shown the world a moving steam engine shifting heavy loads on an iron trackway between Stockton and Darlington.

Yet there were, as always, mixed feelings in the inns. In particular, older men wondered what effect the iron trackway would have on the Turnpike toll road. Every year 20,000 tons of goods, mainly coal, were carried on that long and laborious road to Canterbury. To the younger men, however, this latest

R. Class O-6-OT Locomotive
Whitstable Harbour
1900.

technology offered the prospect of speed and convenience. Instead of taking two hours, the goods could reach the city in a mere forty minutes. To them it was an exciting prospect.

The 3rd of May 1830 dawned sunny, and with bands and bunting, for good or ill, the new future came in, not with a bang, but with much clanking and hissing of steam. The locomotive 'Invicta' had arrived in town - though not from Canterbury. For most of the six-mile journey, the thirty carriages had been moved by a combination of cable, two fixed engines, and gravity. Three hundred passengers had been carried quietly through gentle spring country-side and ancient woodland, with new plant life springing up on embankments and cuttings, and bird song abounding. Only over the last stretch was 'Invicta' powerful enough to haul the train, drown the sounds of nature, and exhibit the power of steam. For that, she was 'loudly cheered by the assembled multitude', as she snorted and puffed and clanked her way from Bogshole to the wooden platform near the dusty harbour excavations.

Behind the brave show of bands and bunting at least some of the passengers must have found it difficult not to feel some honest apprehension mixed with the excitement of the journey, not least through the newly hewn tunnel. Most managed to hide their fear, for a reporter wrote: *'The entrance into the Tunnel was very impressive - total darkness - the accelerated speed - the rumbling of the cars - the loud cheering of the whole party echoing through the vault, combined to form a situation almost certainly novel and striking. Perfect confidence in the safety of the whole apparatus, however, seemed to prevail, and the company of nearly 300 persons emerged from the tunnel into the warm precincts of the cheerful day in high spirits.'*

They were right to be in high spirits, for they were sharing in the birth of modern passenger railways: three hundred men and women had been conveyed in special carriages pulled at least part of the way by a moving steam engine inaugurating a regular daily service. Yet it was a happy event that is strangely ignored by the history books.

Having arrived unscathed in Whitstable the excited passengers got down from the carriages, laughed and smiled at each other, dusted themselves down, and marched to that ancient hostelry, the Duke of Cumberland, for a celebratory luncheon provided by the Railway Company. They made light of the dusty walk in the sunshine along the seawall past the half-completed harbour, and even more happily and noisily they ambled back to the train at five o'clock for the return journey to Canterbury.

Among those travelling on that historic journey must surely have been a certain Mr. Charles Pearson. His father had come to Whitstable from London to supervise his interests in the local 'copperas' industry at Tankerton. This processed a local mineral to produce a chemical then much used in the textile industry to assist dyeing. Wishing to establish himself as a country gentleman he built a house (now become The Castle), purchased the land around and acquired the title 'Lord of the Manor'. Young Mr. Charles inherited both wealth and title, but not all his father's business acumen. He lived in grand style, sometimes in Whitstable, sometimes in a London town-house and before the end of his life was much the poorer. But at this time, 1830, just two years after his father's death, he was a man riding the crest of a wave. He had sold land to the railway and purchased shares in it, and this made him a Director.

Pearson's Arms
Almshouses, Tower Parade

Original 'Pearson's Arms'

Charles Pearson Junior, Lord of the Manor at the Castle, began building a hotel and public house around 1828, anticipating that the railway line would run close by down to jetties from the beach. Alas for him, a harbour was built instead and the line curved away westward. The new establishment was not ready for the grand opening of the railway in 1830, but it was the centre of celebration for that of the harbour in 1832. The position away from the railway station and the harbour meant that the Pearson's Arms did not flourish and it probably closed in the 1840s. Certainly in 1850 the empty building was let to the Coastguard. It must have been about this time that the name was transferred to the beer-house at the Horsebridge.

Pearson's Crab & Oyster House (Pearson's Arms)
The Horsebridge

1845 The Pearson's Arms was advertised for sale in the estate of George Buckley; the licensee was Thomas Barnes. Buckley had also owned the Smack on Middle Wall. The beer-house had acquired the name of the original Pearson's Arms which had been opened by Charles Pearson of the Castle in 1832, on the site of today's almshouses in Tower Parade. By 1840 this had closed. Earlier this beer-house at the Horsebridge may have been called the Whitstable Tavern. It was established in a cottage part of which remains at the rear; it is said to have had a smugglers hideaway under the floor. By 1864 the Pearson's was owned by Ash & Co the Canterbury brewers. In that year the magistrates withheld the license as the Police reported the 'house' to be "conducted very badly", the landlord "harboured loose women

and was in the habit of getting intoxicated himself". The landlord in 1881 also had a problem – he was driven to suicide (by his wife it was said) by sticking his head in the rainwater butt. Probably in 1870 the modern part of the tavern was built and it became a prosperous 'house' with a snug bar, parlour bar, smoke room and club room. It catered especially for the dredgermen who worked from the Horsebridge. In recent years it has gained a particular reputation for sea-food as reflected in the change to the traditional name. It is now a Whitbread's 'house'.

Now he decided to build a hostelry to serve both the harbour and the railway. So, as early as 1828, it became known that *'an additional public house will be opened in Tankerton, Whitstable, in a few days time, called the "Pearson Arms".'*

In fact, it was not until August 1832 that the hotel, the first in Whitstable to be purpose built, was ready. An advertisement described it glowingly.

'Now occupying a most eligible position close to the sea and Railway being an indispensable appendage to the improvement now in progress... with bowling green, gardens, meadows, stabling, etc.'

In spite of the delay, it was ready for the much greater celebration in Whitstable on 19th march 1832. Ten thousand people had come to Whitstable for the opening of the harbour, an important event for this old maritime town.

' The Directors attended by their Friends and the excellent Band of the 7th Dragoon Guards, and about 250 passengers left the Canterbury station, and proceeded at an expeditious rate, to open the Harbour, and upon arrival at Whitstable were received by a salute from the Guns at the Pier Head, and a dense crowd of spectators. The Bay of Whitstable presented a gay and animating appearance being filled with vessels of every denomination, dressed out with their Colours and Flags and their decks crowded with numerous parties. The Directors with the engineers and other officers of the company, forthwith proceeded on board of a vessel engaged for the purpose, and having made a short tack, sailed into the harbour with flying colours, and amid the cheers of the surrounding thousands. The various other Ships and Vessels vied to outdo each other in following the Directors into the Harbour, and several Colliers and other vessels also entered in order to be discharged of their cargoes. Upon the ceremony of opening the Harbour being concluded, the Royal Sovereign Boat, belonging to the Steam Navigation Company, appeared in sight with passengers from London, and it shortly entered in the most majestic style, and with as much ease and confidence as if the Harbour and its entrance had been in constant use by the steersman.'

The passengers having landed, and the formalities ended, the Directors proceeded to *'the New Hotel, called the Pearson Arms, where a very excellent Public Breakfast had been prepared and furnished in good taste.'* Business was brisk, for *'the Hotel was crowded during the whole day, and many of the Visitors remained to dine and pass away a joyous evening.'*

The new hotel started as a real money-spinner for Pearson. In 1833 the newspaper gave its readers a description of the sort of hospitality the place was able to provide, this time of a more personal nature:

'Friday 24th August 1832: 'On Saturday last, Mr. Pearson, eldest son of Charles Pearson, esq., of this town, attained his majority, on which occasion, a party of friends dined together at the Pearsons Arms Hotel where the choicest display of every delicacy of the season were set before them by Mr. Pritchard the landlord. In the evening, a second party was regaled with a repast of roast beef and plum pudding. The morning was ushered in with the

ringing of bells, the hoisting of flags, etc., and in the afternoon there was boat racing and field sports in great variety, interspersed with some excellent performances by the band of the Catch club. In the evening a display of Fireworks was exhibited and the festivities concluded by dancing which was kept up to a late hour.'

The future looked bright. In the 1820s only about 4,000 people used the toll road every year. In 1835, by contrast, 26,000 travelled by rail. Of course, the novelty of the railway wore off, and this huge number was not repeated. Nevertheless, travelling to London from Canterbury by rail and then by sea from the harbour was cheaper, nearly as quick, and in good weather pleasanter than by coach and horses. So for a few year's at least the Pearson's Arms prospered as travellers called there for refreshment and accommodation.

However, it was not long before the brightness began to fade. Pearson found the hotel was not so well placed: the town was not growing as he had hoped and the hotel continued to lie on open undeveloped ground well away from the town centre and beyond the harbour and railway. Then around 1836, coinciding with a new fast boat service to London, an inn, the Steam Packet, was opened at the harbour gates, taking more of his clientele. Indeed Pearson's fortunes reached so low an ebb that he was made bankrupt and forced to sell all his Whitstable estate to Wynn Ellis, another London businessman..

If he could have hung on, things might have been different, for when the railway was modernised in 1846 with locomotives employed throughout, the town did begin to grow, trade increased, and Whitstable began to expand swiftly eastwards towards the harbour and his sadly defunct hotel.

As it was, Wynn Ellis, the new Lord of the manor and owner of the building, leased it to the Coastguard in 1850: around that time the old name somehow became attached to a newly built public house at the Horsebridge: The Pearson's Arms, now the Pearson's Crab and Oyster House. Pearson's original building disappeared when Wynn Ellis built the present-day Almshouses on the site, perhaps using parts of the original structure.

Soil excavated from the harbour had been used to widen the sea wall. This not only made a quay, but also made room, as Pearson found to his chagrin, for an inn to serve railway passengers as well as labourers and railway workers. The Steam Packet opened its doors in about 1836, to coincide with the formation of the Canterbury and Whitstable Steam Packet Company, which set up a regular, though short-lived, thrice-weekly service from London. At first the new inn had but the one bar facing the harbour, but when railway services were improved another bar was added facing the road. Manual

41

Steam Packet
Sea Angling Club, Harbour Street

With the opening of the railway line to Canterbury in 1830 and the harbour in 1832, there were plenty of thirsty men in need of good ale. So it was not long before a beerhouse was built, originally facing towards the harbour. The first licensee noted is Benjamin Harnett in 1838; the brewery which built the weather-boarded pub is not known. In the 1860s an extension was built with the Steam Packet now facing on to the road. Doubtless this reflected the growth of the town towards the harbour. The rear bar was still used by the dusty and dirty labourers and sailors, while the front bars were patronised by travellers and residents. On 9th October 1913 the Steam Packet burnt down, only the brick chimneys remaining. The Steam Packet 'Hotel' was rebuilt by the leasing brewers George Beer & Co of the Star Brewery in Canterbury. In 1950 ownership passed to Fremlins. In 1958 the harbour was bought by the Town Council and in 1962 the public house was closed in order to provide accommodation for the Harbour Master and the Customs Office. The building remains as the home of the Sea Angling Club.

workers in dirty, dusty clothes, kept to the original bar, leaving the new one to cleaner and more respectable customers.

As Whitstable expanded along Harbour Street towards the harbour, more beer-houses appeared: the Spread Eagle and the Royal Native joined the Nelson. Nearby on Sea Wall came the Victoria. Shops and houses were built too, reflecting increasing wealth, particularly in the growth of maritime industries. Although most of the buildings in the area were still the black tar-coated timber fire-traps typical of Whitstable, it was a definite sign of growing prosperity when a substantial block of brick buildings appeared on a narrow site across the road from the harbour on Ludgate Hill in 1863. Here there was a row of shops, a cafe, and in the middle a substantial South-East Railway Hotel, with its ground floor grandly faced with stonework.

The whole area had become busy and thriving, its growth only interrupted by the great fire of 1869, described later, which destroyed the Spread Eagle and the Victoria. Only the latter was rebuilt: it remains today as the headquarters and bar of the Yacht club. On the south side of Harbour Street a terrace had been built and at the end came another public house: the Railway Tavern (now the Punch).

The Steam Packet Inn meanwhile survived and prospered - in its way. For although by the 1880s the respectable side was staging sumptuous club dinners, the rougher harbour-facing side had a somewhat different character, one which was shared with neighbouring hostelries. For the whole area had become the haunt of rip-roaring sea-farers and labourers from the town, foreign sailors from Scandinavia on the loose, and prostitutes from who-knew-where. All combined to ensure raucous scenes of drunkenness, violence, and public-disorder. It was not unusual for drunken men to be hauled from the harbour severely injured and nearly suffocated with mud, while policemen trying to make arrests were knocked down and kicked, with other members of the customer's crew joining in the fray and bystanders watching with interest the struggle with the forces of law and order.

Then the Steam Packet, too, was destroyed by fire in 1912, rebuilt, and converted to other uses in the 1950s, remaining today a centre for local anglers. As harbour trade declined, the block containing the South East Railway Hotel

---

Royal Native
No 19 Harbour Street

This was a small beer-house which existed from around 1875. It was owned by Flint and Sons, the Canterbury brewers and closed around 1908. It is now a shop.

Lord Nelson
49 Harbour Street

This public house occupied originally an old property probably dating to the late seventeenth century. In the early 1800s it was described as a house, stable, coalyard with shop belonging to Henry Hunt. Previous occupiers had been Jacob Tevelin and William Rowbottom. On Hunt's death in 1811 the property was held in Trust for his wife and family, with a complex settlement involving the Carey and Frend families by marriages. 1876 they sold the Lord Nelson to Canterbury brewer A. J. Beer who was already leasing the building, for £130. Probably the beerhouse had been established in the 1860s, responding to the rapid growth of housing in the streets south of Harbour Street, the 'new town' as it was then called. By 1894 the pub had passed to the Original Brewery of Alfred Walton & Co of Westerham. They demolished the dilapidated buildings and erected the present one at a cost of £800. As one of the 'modern' pubs in the town the Lord Nelson prospered. It was noted for its food - breakfasts, teas and suppers - and became the home of a number of clubs. In 1962 ownership passed to Ind Coope and then other major brewers, until having suffered a great decline it was closed by the Public Health Department in 1981. 1987 the building was purchased by the City Council and became their local offices in Whitstable.

became derelict and was finally demolished in 1965. Recently the area, known as Starvation Point, has been landscaped.

Today only the Punch Tavern survives to remind Whitstable of the men who manned its historic railway and once-bustling harbour and the rough days of demon drink.

South-Eastern Railway Tavern
Starvation Point (Ludgate Hill).

1863 Thomas Gann bought the narrow strip of ground between New Street and Harbour Road from Wyn Ellis, Lord of the Manor. Thomas Porter was employed to build two blocks of buildings, one facing down Harbour Street, and the other looking towards the Harbour. This end of the town was now growing rapidly with the terraced streets extending off Harbour Street and trade was booming at the harbour itself. So, in the centre of the side block a large and handsome tavern was built: three storeys and attics and the ground-floor facade faced with stonework. This was the South-eastern Railway Tavern. It flourished during the late Victorian period but declined after the First World War as harbour trade reduced. The tavern closed in 1927 and became a private house. It revived as a social centre again during the Second World War as a Toc-H centre for troops and a British Restaurant for civilians. The building became empty again and indeed gradually the whole block became derelict and it was demolished in the 1960s. Now this triangle of land has been landscaped by the Improvement Trust; an information board there has an illustration of the tavern building.

Starvation Point

Punch Tavern (Railway Tavern)
Harbour Street

George Cox erected a block of five tenements in the 1820s as part of the expansion of Harbour Street. The end property remained a house for some years but probably in the 1850s Stephen Perkins established a beer-house there. He is first listed as such in 1858. This was of course a good position near to the harbour and the Canterbury railway line. 1863 Perkins bought the property for £500. By 1865 he had built two houses next door at the beginning of Harbour Place (now Woodlawn Street), undertaking a mortgage with Flints the Canterbury brewery; part of one house remains today as the slate-roofed end of the pub. At this time there were other buildings in front to a much narrower Harbour Street, and this shielded the tavern from the destruction caused by the great fire of 1869. In 1882 Perkins, who had remained the landlord, sold the tavern to George Carvell of Whitstable, probably on behalf of Flint & Co. who then became the eventual owners. As a result of brewery amalgamation it has become a Whitbread's 'house'.

5 SHIPYARDS & DIVERS

Ask visitors to Whitstable what sticks in their memory of the place, and the chances are they'll mention the Old Neptune. This modest pub is certainly a memorable building, standing as it does isolated and foursquare at the edge of the beach, scorning the protection of nearby Island Wall.

The Neptune's solitary position makes it one of the attractive features of the Whitstable waterfront, and is a favourite scene much painted by local artists. Almost invariably they feature a sunny summer's day, with the greys and browns of the beach contrasting with the blue and white buildings and the blue of the sky. The wide beach they paint is intersected by sturdy groynes against which people sprawl at their ease in summer sun, their placid peace broken only by the clink of glasses, the voices of children or the sound of racket on tennis ball.

But in the nineteenth century the scene was very different, for it was here and along Island Wall that ships' carpenters, encouraged by this broad uncluttered sweep of shore, prospered, their workshops growing into small

shipyards with slipways running down to the sea. The original Neptune was itself a boat building shop, and nearby cottages housed workmen and their families. It was altogether a busy scene; Whitstable was a thriving maritime town, and the working men - dredgermen, shipbuilders, divers - need refreshment during the day and a place to meet in the evenings away from those cramped cottages often crowded with young children. Several public houses therefore rapidly developed along the Island Wall. At the very far end, and only to be reached along the top of the sea-wall, was the Star, a beer-house in one of the small cottages. Like the others it prospered because a shipyard was developed nearby. Today it remains as a private house.

One of the new inns was the Guinea also now a private residence, situated near where grandly named Waterloo Place met the sea-wall. The story of its building is uniquely contained in letters from its first licensee, William Pettman, to his son Daniel in Australia. After Daniel's death, the letter's were found and returned to the family in Whitstable.

In April 1861, Mr. Pettman described how he planned to pull down the old

Star
151 Island Wall

In 1792 the Island Wall was constructed and the Salts behind drained. Edward Foad, one of the schemes promoters sold a plot of land lying on the landward side of the Wall in 1803 to George Walker for £22-10s, and there he built a cottage. In 1832 Walker sold to Thomas Starr, an attorney of Canterbury. The cottage then changed hands a number of times and was split into two tenements. When purchased by George Blaxland in 1870 it was again a single dwelling and here the beer-house 'The Star' was established, the licensee being John Dyason. Although in a very isolated position reached only by the narrow track along the sea-wall, there was at this time a shipyard relatively close to provide an adequate living. In 1911 it closed and Neames, the Faversham brewers, then the owners, sold to Alfred Daniels of the Shipping Company and the old cottage was extended to make quite a large house. For some years it was owned by the son of Lord Fisher of Lambeth (the former Archbishop) who frequently visited there.

forge which had stood there, building a new one at the rear, and a beer house fronting Island Wall. In December he wrote: *'We have a good settle [scullery] with a 6 foot pitch and a good spring of water underneath which I bored besides the old spring. We have also 4 rooms, above 2 rooms, downstairs 2 rooms 8' - 6' pitch, 4 bedrooms. A large bar parlour. Built of as good bricks as could be had. The front has two large bow windows, the front door is glass.'* It was profitable: *'We at present sell 3 barrels per week which leaves a profit of about 17/- per barrel, beside the spirit which we began to sell on 11th October.'* A photograph survives, which shows Mr. Pettman outside his happily flourishing business, *'the only free public house in Whitstable,'* which he reckoned to be worth £1000.

Things continued well. Two years later, while still reporting good profits, he describes a town at ease with itself, and thriving, *'It is a very orderly house, no bad company uses here,'* he wrote, and, *'Whitstable is now very flourishing, new streets and building everywhere. New houses building and its nearly full up from the Turnpike up to above the Two Brewers. Up to Old Jack Anderson's Cross Way Post. We have also four slipways close to me which makes trade very brisk. There are nearly always ships on them of late.'*

It's not certain where the name 'Guinea', possibly unique in England, came

Guinea Inn
No 31 Island Wall

1850s William Pettman owned a cottage and forge here. 1861 he moved the forge to the backyard and fronting his cottage built a brick house with a bar parlour opening to the road. It opened in the April as the only 'free house' in the town. It flourished with trade from nearby shipyards. Traditionally Pettman is said to have made money earlier from smuggling golden guineas across to the continent.

The pub was later bought by Flint & Co of Canterbury. It enjoyed a good reputation for clubs and outings. From 1967 the Jaffas ran entertainments with jazz bands and popular drag acts. The pub was closed by Whitbread's in 1981 and it is now a private house.

from. William Pettman doesn't explain. One tradition associates it with Whitstable's long history of smuggling. Guineas were often smuggled across to France, but this was much earlier in the century, and most commonly from Deal and Folkestone. Another tradition links the name with golden guineas brought back to Whitstable by divers working on Spanish Galleons.

There's certainly a whiff of treasure trove pervading the whole area. The terrace of six small cottages nearby, Copeland Cottages, better known as Dollar Row, is often said to have been built from the proceeds of treasure. If true, this came not from a Spanish Armada galleon, but more probably from the 'Enterprise', a slave ship carrying home fruit and £40,000 in silver dollars which sank in 1803 near the Copeland Islands off NW Ireland. The connection is further underlined in the name of the residence at the end, Copeland House, where Thomas Gann lived. His son John certainly worked on the 'Enterprise' wreck and a descendant of his treasures a silver dollar. It is a coin blackened by pitch, surely an indication that it might truly have been smuggled to Whitstable hidden in a tar-barrel. Like many a smuggling tale, it's a matter of hearsay, nods and winks.

But such stories do certainly show that Whitstable men at this time were travelling far, for they were pioneers in the diving industry. They developed a world-wide reputation, some of them being sent for from as far afield as the

West Indies. Indeed, as Hollingshead wrote, *'if it had not fallen to the lot of Whitstable to be celebrated for its oysters, and its company of "free-dredgers" it might have claimed a word of notice for producing the rarest of all workmen, the sea-diver.'*

Those that travelled furthest, a special group, centred themselves when in town at 'The Kings Head', next to Dollar Row. As the Duke of Cumberland had once been the centre for oyster-dredgers, so this tavern became a centre for the divers.

For sixty and more years, these men were very much a part of the maritime scene of Whitstable. Tradition attributes the invention of diving apparatus with a helmet and air supply to local man John Deane. The story goes that he dramatically rescued some horses from a burning stable at Downs farm by using the helmet from a suit of old armour in the hallway with air being supplied by a pump that had been used for hosing the fire. What is quite certain is that his brother Charles had already invented a breathing apparatus for entering smoke-filled rooms, and a similar primitive apparatus was used by the brothers in salvage work in shallow water. In 1830 the brothers met George

King's Head
No 18 Island Wall

In 1830 James Daniels bought the ground fronting the sea wall and developed a shipwrights's workshop. By 1855, now leasing the Whitstable brewery, Daniels sold off the ground in seven building plots. Thomas Gann who lived in nearby Copeland House and had built the adjoining terrace (Dollar Row), bought two and built the house which became the Kings Head Public House. 1859 Edward Appleton, the first licensee, bought the property for £780. The pub became the social centre for divers working for John Gann. 1871 bought by Robert Frend, and after some years of leasing it was purchased by Flints, brewers of Canterbury. 1911 described as in poor condition, it was closed. The Kings Head became a private house and was given the pedimented facade and the grand doorway.

Doorway detail.

Hall, a bell diver who suggested using the force pump to push air in at the top of the helmet. So the technique developed, and with it the local industry. Although John Deane moved to Portsmouth in 1832 with William Edwards (where they worked on the wreck of the 'Royal George' and discovered the 'Mary Rose'), Thomas Gann and George Bell, having acquired Deane's apparatus, continued to work from Whitstable. A number of local men gained diving experience and by 1856, John Gann and Alfred Gann had four salvage boats which maintained a group of about a dozen men. Their experience was recognised world wide in salvaging from sunken vessels and in using explosives in removing dangerous wrecks. The divers were very active in World War One, but after the war, the business failed in the face of more advanced apparatus being developed on the Continent. So the industry died, but Whitstable remembers its men.

For they were tough. *'These men go to work in the diving dress, until they are sixty or seventy years of age. The dress consists of a water-proof body suit, to keep them dry and warm; very heavily-weighted boots, to keep them steady and on their legs; and the well-known helmet with the glass-eye windows, which is furnished with air pumped from the boat above down the elastic tube.'*

They were brave. *'He may have got the precious casket, to which he has been directed, in his arms; but what of that, if he die before he find the stairs?'*

The Fisherman's Arms
34 Island Wall

The background of this property has not been traced. Cottages along Island Wall tended to be built from the 1840s onwards as ship-repairing and construction spread along the beach. This beer-house is noted in 1858 as the Fishmonger's Arms (perhaps a misprint?) with Elizabeth Bell as licensee. Earlier in 1845 a George Bell is listed by name only; this may have been her husband. This suggests a likely beginning for the beer-house about 1840. William Madams advertised in 1860 that he had altered and extended the 'house' to "make it a hotel". This improvement may have included the brick front with its Dutch-style gable. In 1903, owned by Shepherd Neame it was one of a number of small pubs recommended for closure and this took place around 1906. The Fisherman's Arms then became a private house.

asked the landsman Hollingshead, *'But we never think about risk,'* replied the diver: *'Were we once to take to considering what our risks are - how the least neglect above, the least accident below, might make dead men of us - why, I daresay there would be a good many who'd knock off. A man wants nerves for the work, and nerves don't allow thinking.'*

And so they showed mental toughness too. In the dark and cold of a rotting wreck, a diver might know that *'the cold helpless masses that bump against his helmet, as they float along the low roof over his head, are the decomposed corpses of those who were huddled together in the cabin when the ship went down. A few of these may be on the floor under his feet, but only pinned down by an overturned table or a fallen chest. Their tendency is upward - ever upward - and the remorseless sea washes away the dead infant from it's dead mother's arms, the dead wife from her husband's embrace.'* Was it any wonder, then, that such men needed a place like the King's Head in which to be able to talk a language only they understood? Perhaps it is not the whiff of treasure that pervades Island Wall so much as the ghostly memories of 'green ribs and timbers covered with barnacles and weed, and who knew what else beside.'

Copland House and Dollar Row

6 FROM STREET TO TOWN

We saw earlier how the trackway to the city of Canterbury encouraged the growth of the tiny community of Whitstable. More and more shipping in the bay, more movement of cargo between boats and shore, more waggoners with teams of horses - all this meant more taverns and beer-houses along the straggling street that led towards Canterbury.

In early days the beer came from Canterbury, and the ale-houses themselves were usually owned by city men. As Whitstable grew in size and prosperity so some of the newer 'houses', were set up by local people. But still the pace of change remained slow, and it was many years before a local brewery appeared.

It happened this way. Mid-eighteenth century property deeds show that there was a forge alongside the roadway opposite today's library. In a progression typical of Whitstable, the 1778 owner, John Saunders, expanded it into a coalyard, and with a supply of fuel, and hops coming by from

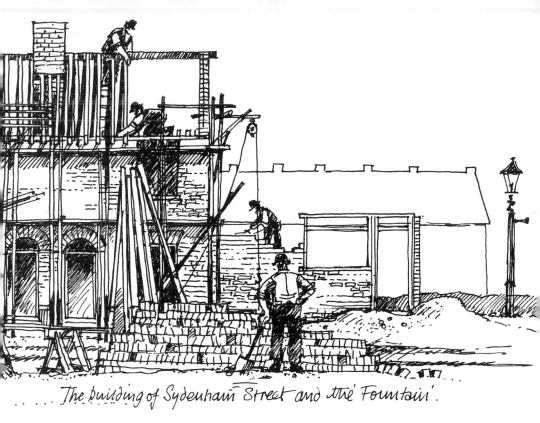

..... The building of Sydenham Street and the 'Fountain'.

Canterbury for export, it was an easy step for him or his son, another John, to start brewing beer. As the business prospered, the nearby East Kent Tavern was established, catering for respectable travellers and residents.

Early in the nineteenth century the house and brewhouse, some land and a cottage were sold to a Seasalter farmer, William Hopper, and he put in a tenant, James Daniels, formerly a shipwright on Island Wall. Hopper's 1847 will describes the property as 'brewhouse, malthouse, stable, plant, steam engine, utensils, implements.' In 1850 four cottages - Cliff Terrace - were built for the workers at the rear of the brewery on what is now West Cliff, together with Trafalgar House, a villa for the Master Brewer. The site had developed into a neatly self-contained little industrial unit.

When Hopper died in 1852 a sale at the Bear & Key offered this *'very compact Brewhouse with Plant Dwelling House and garden, Coalyard, Stables, Cart Lodges and Outhouses. The brewhouse is an old established one, with ale and porter cellars, is in excellent condition and fitted with a Four Horse Power Steam Engine... a malt mill and all modern appliances necessary for carrying on an extensive business and is now in full trade.'* The house faced the road and was double-fronted with ten rooms. This sale did not include the cottages and villa but even without these, the sale realised £1000 when it was bought by James Daniels, the sitting tenant. To cope with his expenses he himself had to sell off a site on Island wall, bought by Thomas Gann, on which the latter straightaway built the King's Head.

Daniels' two sons inherited when he died in 1857, and in 1866 they sold the ninety-year old business to the Canterbury brewer George Johnson. By this time the coal trade had moved to the harbour with its railway connection, and with brewing being a major industry in the city Johnson closed the local brewery and the site was sold for building. Just down the road was the Brewery Tap, a small frontage built on to an old cottage with strong smuggling associations, and the new brewer maintained this outlet.

During all this time, commerce and industry were flourishing as never before. The fleet in the bay comprised upwards of 70 vessels trading in coastal and foreign waters; shipbuilding and repairing were at full stretch; the divers were engaged on many vessels and worked for the Government in the Crimea during the war, and the oyster industry reached its peak with the insatiable demand of the London market where oysters sustained the poor as well as satisfying the rich.

Whitstable prospered and soon gained those public buildings and amenities which gave it the dignity of a town. From the 1840's to the '60s appeared its church and several handsome chapels; there was a Trust school and a private commercial academy; a bank was opened and a local newspaper launched; a Police Station was built and gas lighting introduced. The Assembly Rooms were built, providing a centre for public entertainment and town meetings, and the main railway line arrived linking Whitstable directly through to London.

It was, indeed, the nineteenth century which saw the greatest development of Whitstable, as the map of 1872 shows. At the start of the century the population was little more than 1000. By 1841 it had risen to more than 3000, and in each of the next three decades it went up by 1000, and the number of dwellings increased from 700 to around 1100. The swiftness of change is well illustrated in those letters the Pettmans of the Guinea inn wrote to their son in Australia. In 1855 they told him: *'A great many houses built near Harbour Street called Sydenham Street and also Swan Terrace...'* Three years later: *' Whitstable is now in a very flourishing state a great many new houses being built... they are building very fast down the Island so that you scarcely know*

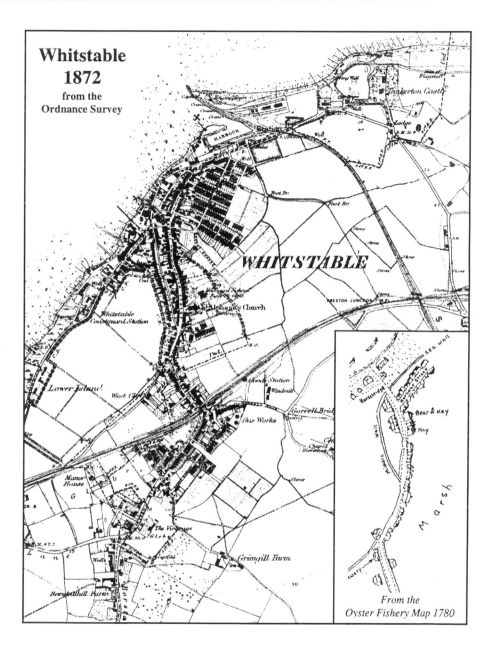

Whitstable 1872
from the Ordnance Survey

From the Oyster Fishery Map 1780

Whitstable...' In 1863, 'Whitstable is now very flourishing, new streets and buildings everywhere... it's nearly full up from the turnpike to above the Two Brewers', and the following year Mr. Pettman reported 'the town continues to

The 'New Town' Pubs
Horn of Plenty, Albert Street
Forester's Arms, 60 Albert Street
Fountain, 29 Sydenham Street
Sovereign, 45 Victoria Street
Globe , 7 Victoria Street
New Inn (Bricklayers Arms), 30 Woodlawn Street

New Inn

From the 1840s as Whitstable prospered and the population grew the demand for more housing was largely met by an estate development on the south side of Harbour Street. A grid-pattern of parallel streets was laid out and gradually filled with terraced housing occupied by the newly prosperous oyster dredgers, mariners and shipyard craftsmen. These working men required their 'local' in which to spend a convivial evening away from homes often crowded with children. So beer-houses, as they were then called, were established, strategically sited at the street intersections.

The Horn of Plenty was apparently a short-lived beer-house when Albert Street had only just started to develop; its location has not been identified.

In 1844/45 John Gibbens and George Rigden of Canterbury owned a block of land in this area, presumably as a speculation. They now sold four 13-foot plots to James Kelson, a builder: Lots 13 and 14 on Harbour Place (now Woodlawn Street), and Lots 41 and 42 on Sydenham Street. The first two he sold on to Henry Cornelius of Whitstable who built two houses and the end one became a beer-house, the Bricklayer's Arms. This had rather a rough reputation in its early days, so it may have been that, or perhaps the name seemed out-moded, that by 1894 it had been changed to the New Inn, as it remains today. In 1896 it was sold to Neames of Faversham.

It was not until 1862 that houses were built on the two plots at the end of Sydenham Street, by a local bricklayer John Bushell. The end one became the Fountain Inn, which was bought by Alfred Wood in 1866; he had leased the property though several years earlier. As with all local pubs it was bought by a brewery, here Johnson & Co. of the Northgate Brewery and by later amalgamations it became part of the Ind Coope group. Unusually, in 1982 it reverted to being a 'free house'.

Sovereign

The Globe probably opened in the 1850's and the Sovereign and Forester's in the next decade. The Sovereign became a Rigden's Pub and happily still retains their inscribed window glass. The Foresters was closed in the early seventies and is now a private house. In the survey of 1903 all these 'New Town' pubs were noted as "well conducted", reflecting the respectability of the terraced streets. By this time the Globe had closed. The site of the Globe, at the junction of Regent Street and Victoria Street disappeared one Autumn day. On the 11th October 1941, a single German bomber came out of the sun and dropped one huge bomb right on this spot. There was a vast crater and devastation over a wide area, though only three lives were lost. Next day troops were brought in to help clear the debris. A splendid spirit of 'not being down-hearted' prevailed, many were the stories of lucky escapes and humour abounded. Two young soldiers gaped at the vast hole and asked what they should do, "well, you can try your hands at filling it", a local replied! Today the area is covered by a car-park.

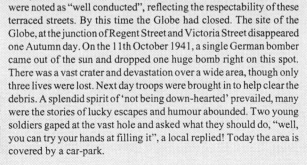

Fountain

increase in size. I hardly know where I am when I go down to the new part of the town called Victoria and Albert Streets and Bexley Place and Bexley Street. They keep building as fast as they can...' He was describing an extraordinary building boom.

This expansion in the 1850s created what was virtually a new town area. It was here between Harbour Street and Oxford Street that a grid of intersecting roads was laid out and blocks of terraced houses built, extending in stages from Harbour Street. At the intersection of many of the streets purpose-built pubs formed focal points for custom and socialising, catering for the new artisan class. There was the short-lived Horn of Plenty on Albert Terrace, probably replaced by the Foresters Arms as the terrace extended into Albert Street. On Victoria Street was the Globe, long closed by 1941, when the site was flattened by a World War Two bomb; on Harbour Place (now Woodlawn Street) there was the Bricklayers Arms later the New Inn, while on Sydenham Street there was the Fountain, and in St. Peter's Street the Sovereign. Only the last three survive today.

New pubs were not confined to these terraced streets. Licensed premises proliferated in the older parts of the town as well. Near the Horsebridge the established inns, the Bear & Key, Duke of Cumberland and the Red Lion soon found themselves surrounded by lesser establishments. Two small timber built beer-houses, the Stag and the Dredgermen's Arms, appeared on the Sea

Stag
Stag Cottage, Sea Wall

John Deane and William Edwards, the pioneers in diving apparatus and methods, purchased ground along the Valley Wall, as it was then called, in 1853. Here they built a store for their equipment, and it is said they also kept here for a time some of the cannons which they had raised from the Royal George and the Mary Rose in the Solent. In 1858 they sold the property to Rest Flint, the Canterbury brewer for £155. The first licensee of the beer-house was John Anderson. At some stage the brewers added the brick front to the original weather-board building. In 1903 it was described as "a small pokey house"; it had just a single bar, but it was found to be exceptionally clean and the landlord was an excellent cook (so even such a small place served food). Flint & Sons still owned the pub. With very limited trade the Stag closed in 1906 and became a private house.

Alberres (Prince Albert)
Red Lion Lane

Details for this building have not been found. The original weatherboard building was first noted as a beer-house in 1874 with, Frederick Ruck as landlord. In 1903 it was owned by Mrs Emily Holden, one of the only 'free houses' in the town. It had a bar and bar-parlour, five bedrooms; it was described as "dirty and badly constructed for licensed premises". It was shortly after sold to Shepherd Neame who then built the present premises. In 1938 William Joyce alias 'Lord Haw-Haw' used to drink here after haranguing the crowd across the way. In more recent times the pub has become a wine bar. In the drawing is Brownings Yard on the left with a typical wagon which plied from the Horsebridge to Canterbury

Alma
No 2 Middle Wall

This was the end property of the early nineteenth century terrace. Named after the Crimean War battle of 1854, it was first noted as a beerhouse in 1858, the first licensee; William Solly. It was well placed for trade at the road junction and opposite Holloway's shipyard (now the site of the car park). But by 1900 there were seven other licensed premises within 120 yards including the town's major establishments. Owned by Flint & Co of Canterbury, it now catered for local fishermen and sailors; as always with this brewery, the landlord was a retired mariner. With declining trade the Alma closed in 1911, and it returned to being a private house. Later this was removed for road widening.

60

wall. The former probably incorporated the workshop of William Edwards and John Deane, those inventive and innovative Whitstable divers. This was sold to Canterbury brewers Flint & Sons in 1859 and they added the brick facade seen in the building today. Both premises were small but certainly by the time of a survey made in 1903 they had sharply contrasting characters: the Dredgermen's Arms said to badly supervised and dirty, catering for the 'roughest classes': the Stag well conducted and very clean - yet what was a male skeleton, discovered in 1953, doing buried at its back door? Murder? A smuggler's revenge? Who can tell?

Below Sea Wall across Brownings Yard where the Horsebridge cart-horses were stabled was another timber built beer-house, the Prince Albert (now in 1993 called Alberre's). This was rather larger, with two bars; it too was described in 1903 as 'dirty and badly constructed for licensed premises'.

Smack and Wall Tavern
Middle Wall

After the building of the Island Wall in 1792 the Salts behind could be drained. From 1798 it became possible to build cottages on this land below the Middle Wall. Two of these were converted to beer-houses some time after 1830.

Smack

1799 John Nutt, one of the promoters of the draining scheme, sold land to John Knott, who built a cottage there which he then sold in 1808 to John Buckley. 1845 the Buckley family sold the property to John Whorlow, a mariner, for £111. It may be that Whorlow was already in occupation and acting as a beer retailer, certainly he is so listed in 1847. He built another cottage on to the rear of the beer-house and on his death in 1869 both were sold to John Stroud. Percy Neame bought the property in 1880 and added the cottage on the south side in 1889.

Following very critical comments by the magistrates in 1903: "very bad all round, not at all adapted for a public house", Neames rebuilt the Smack on the much larger site now available.

Wall Tavern

1824 the land was purchased by George Bell and here he built a cottage. Very probably he established the beer-house, for his name is listed in 1845. After several other owners the property was leased by Canterbury brewers Flint & Co. in 1865 and they ultimately purchased it. The Wall Tavern, the original weather-board cottage with a modern extension at the front, is now a Whitbread's 'house'.

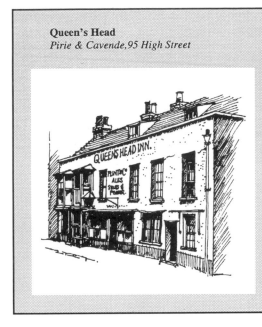

Queen's Head
Pirie & Cavende, 95 High Street

This beerhouse was established in the centre property of an old tenement block, probably dating to the late seventeenth century and owned by the Whitstable Ecclesiastical Charities. William Butcher is first noted here as a beer-retailer in 1845. There were stables at the rear and this may explain the other activities of the next licensees, the Salters. Samuel in 1855 is listed as also a coalmerchant, and John (probably his son) was additionally licensed in 1858 to supply horses for the postal service. In 1871 John styled the establishment 'Queen Anne's Eating House', though it soon reverted to the Queen's Head Inn. The property was leased by Flint & Sons, the Canterbury brewers, and it included the small shop next door on the right. Like many other centre town pubs, trade declined with the changing character of the High Street and the Queen's Head closed in 1912. It is now Pirie & Cavenders bookshop. In the mid-Victorian period the property on the left was the town's first bookshop and stationers run by a schoolmaster, Thomas Tuddenham.

used to harangue his local blackshirts and abusive onlookers from the steps of an old warehouse nearby. Soon afterwards he departed for Germany to take up his notorious career as the broadcaster Lord Haw-Haw, with his anti-British propaganda which always started 'Jairmany calling, Jairmany calling...'

Flint and Sons owned these three houses, and also the Alma at the junction of Middle Wall and Island Wall, now swept away by road widening. This had but the one bar, catered for dredgermen and sailors and probably did rather poorly, with no less than seven other 'houses' within 120 yards. Two still existing are the Wall Tavern and the Smack on Middle Wall. One short-lived beer-house was the Lower Hope which had been situated between the entrance to the Bear & Key and the Hoy (Hatchard's shop now occupies the site).

Away down the High Street from this collection of drinking places centred on The Cross there was the Queen's Head (now Pirie and Cavender's) and across the street a white timber cottage housed a beer-house called the King William. Nearby for a short time was the Reform. Beyond the church an older inn, the Ship, (later the Ship Centurion) survived from the previous century. Deeds suggest there was a coalyard here in the eighteenth century before the inn was established by John Hopper of Seasalter, probably a relation of the

Coach and Horses
Oxford Street

This beer-house began in the end tenement of a row of old cottages which may date to the eighteenth century. In the 1830's the property was owned by John Anderson who was probably the first licensee. It then passed to Charlotte Anderson and then her sister Emma Rye. At some time the beer-house was extended into the cottage adjoining. The Coach and Horses Inn is named in the directory for 1858. Charles Cooper was an early landlord, and later there was Frederick Ruck. The inn was auctioned at the Bear & Key in 1882 and bought by Percy Neame of Faversham for £430. In its prime there were four bars, stabling at the rear, and a popular skittle alley. A later landlord, Percival Humphrey was at the Coach and Horses for 40 years from 1922, one of the town's longest serving landlords. Today it still retains a separate 'snug' bar. It continues today as a Shepherd Neame 'house'.

brewer. The old timber and thatch buildings at the rear remained, and were used to maintain trade in 1913 when Flints were replacing the old building with the more modern premises seen today.

Beyond this, the Coach and Horses was converted from the end house of

King William
22 Oxford Street

Thomas Culver who owned this cottage died in 1805 and the property went to his daughter Elizabeth, wife of Charles Pelfrey (or Pelfry). When Charles died in 1855 his widow Elizabeth then opened a beer-house, the King William (then listed as 82 High Street). It is first noted in 1861. Widows frequently ran public houses, perhaps more usually on the decease of their husband who was the licensee. As the cottage was only 13 feet wide it must have been a very small 'house'. King William IV, known as 'Sailor Billy', enjoyed great popularity during his short reign and numerous pubs were named after him. Elizabeth died in 1867; the public house was now continued by her daughter Mrs. Elizabeth Lewis, until 1878. With her death the property was sold to Osborne Nicholls who lived next door at No 24. It became a private house occupied for the next forty years by Mrs. Jutson.

East Kent
Oxford Street

1802 the house was built by John Saunders the Younger, owner of the Whitstable brewery (located opposite today's Library). 1803 sold to the Horton family of Ashford. 1860 leased by Daniels brothers then owners of the brewery.The tavern was established and suitably named to catch the railway trade of the newly arrived London line, serving East Kent, in 1860. The station was then on the nearby railway bridge. The East Kent was leased later by Johnson & Co. of Canterbury and then sold in 1883 to Neame's of Faversham. Then called an hotel; the railway cabbies kept their horses and traps there. The interior was modernised in 1980.

Beyond this, the Coach and Horses was converted from the end house of a row of cottages. Deeds show that the roadway here was then a mere eleven feet wide, and bordered by a deep ditch that acted as a drain and sewer: altogether it may have been a hazardous undertaking to gain entry for a drink - and perhaps even more hazardous when leaving in the dark. Today at the side is preserved one of the town's first gas lamps: here the school access once led to Sanders Farm on which Cromwell Road was built.

A little distance beyond, there was the East Kent Tavern, mentioned earlier, always known as a superior establishment with accommodation and stables. After the London railway came through in 1860 cabbies used to stable their horses there, for the station then was immediately above the railway bridge close by. During the First World War a local man, George Harman, on the run from the military police, dashed into the East Kent with the military policemen hot on his heels. He grabbed the top hat and long coat of one of the cabbies, unhitched a waiting cab and drove down the High street, horse's nose-bag flying, to escape on a boat at the harbour. This was a typical Whitstable

Noah's Ark
Canterbury Road

This beerhouse was established in an old weatherboard cottage which lay back some sixty feet from the roadway. The owner in 1843 was Edward Duncan. The following year he mortgaged the property with George Buckley who was much involved with setting up beerhouses, so this may indicate the beginning of the Noah's Ark. 1845 the property was sold to R & G Chipperfield for £225, a sum which indicated more than just a cottage was involved. 1852 the beer-house was purchased by William Beer a Canterbury brewer. The licensee in 1858 was William Blackman who was also a coalmerchant. 1871 mortgages amounting to £650 were taken over by St Augustines College in Canterbury, a somewhat surprising investment for a religious institution. Probably in 1872 the present inn on the street line and joining on to the terrace, was built. During the 60s and 70s new housing was beginning to spread along the main road and behind on Swanfield. The pub was bought by the Westerham brewery Bushell & Co. in 1897, and sold to Inde Coupe in 1962. It is now a Whitbread's 'house'.

'cocking a snook' at authority - well worthy of smugglers' traditions.

Where the new railway, linking the town directly with London, crossed the main road there was originally the toll-house and gate of the Turnpike to Canterbury, and a small beer shop kept by Mrs. Madams. The opening of the railway was cause for celebration, and with conviviality the order of the day, no doubt Mrs Madams did well that day and later, for it was not long before her son was encouraged to build a smart new front for what then became the Railway Inn. This was also an area of new building. On the town side of the bridge was the long Hartsfield Terrace. A little way along the country lane that

Rising Sun
Harwich Street

This small public house on Harwich Street was built in the 1860s by Brewers Shepherd Neame to serve the terraced houses along Essex Street and Swanfield Road. Since these had been built a decade or more earlier the pub does not occupy the typical end of terrace position, but was built along the road to the rear, standing on its own. Indeed for many years there was nothing beyond the Rising Sun but the fields.

Golden Lion
Belmont Road (Mill Road)

Details of this property have not been traced. The original weather-board cottage probably dates from the 1840s. A beer-house in Mill Road is listed in 1855, with Thomas Browning as landlord. This 'house' may well have begun under the name of the White Swan, for one is listed for Church Road (the later name for Mill Road) in 1858. Tradition recalls that there was indeed a large pond in the field to the rear which had swans, and this gave the name Swan Field. The name Golden Lion is first noted in 1870. It was later owned by Flints, the Canterbury brewers, and they may well have added the brick frontage. Apparently the pub had a great reputation as the last port-of-call for the farm labourers going home along the country lane on a Saturday night. Here they would gather strength to stagger home, laden with bottles stuffed in their pockets. In 1903 the Golden Lion drew much of its trade from local workers at the railway siding and the gas-works; and here football teams changed for matches on the Belmont ground - doubtless returning to drink to success or defeat! Today it is a Whitbread's 'house'.

led to Church Street (now Belmont Road) the Golden Lion was built, prospering by and catering for workers from the railway goods siding and, later on, the nearby gas works. Other terraces were built off the Canterbury Road and in 1872 the beer-house the Noah's Ark was replaced with new premises fronting the road. New streets were also developed on the east side, and being then a little out of town and so regarded as rather 'respectable' areas, only one public house was established: the Rising Sun.

So the pattern and character of Whitstable's public houses was set during the nineteenth century, in which all sections of the community from humblest to richest were duly catered for. With the exception of the few superior establishments they were very local, catering for nearby working men by day and the neighbouring street or two in the evening.

There was indeed a tremendous growth in the number of public houses in Whitstable in the nineteenth century, brought about, as in the country at large, by a population explosion which increased numbers from around 1,000 inhabitants at the beginning of the century to almost 6,000 by the 1871 census. In addition, beer-drinking became an essential tradition and way of life of the working class, whose work was often hard and arduous. Men, and women, drank hard just to keep going, and later drank to recover. Their homes were often small and cramped and crowded with children, and men found solace in their 'local', in which there was often the need to prove one's manliness by being able to 'hold one's liquor'. In spite of that, the local often became a rough kind of community centre, often bonding together men who worked in a

66

particular industry or trade. There they might play cards or skittles, or just sit and smoke, or, increasingly as their years went by, just gossip and reminisce.

Two more pubs must be mentioned, both of which lay away from the growing town.

On the higher ground to the east was the ancient hamlet of cottages and farms by All Saints Church. Opposite there is still today the Monument public

---

Lower Hope
9 High Street

Details of this beer-house have not been traced, so it must have existed for a short time after 1830 when the new Act allowed beer-houses to be opened. The building itself probably dates from the eighteenth century; it is now Hatchards shop.

Reform
site unknown

This public house is only known from a couple of incidental references. A document of 1849 refers to a drainage pipe running "from Daniels Brewery past the Post Office to the Reform Public House". This provides some clue: the brewery was opposite our Library and the Post Office was at No 3 Oxford Street (next to the museum). So the Reform must have been around the High Street junction with Middle Wall.

Church Street Beer-House

The location of this beer-house is the then tiny hamlet of Church Street and has not been found. James Wood is noted as beer retailer and boot and shoe maker in 1845 and 1855.

Swanfield Terrace
Canterbury Road

Swanfield Terrace is the group of white weatherboard cottages just beyond the railway bridge, on Canterbury Road. Here James Attwood is listed between 1851 and 1861 as beer retailer and brewer. No further information has been found.

Swanfield Terrace

---

house which was established in 1731. A little later it was owned by the same John Cantis who had the Bear & Key down in the town. Church Street was an important focal point with the parish church and an annual Midsummer fair.

The other pub, perhaps, owed its existence to an 1884 outbreak of smallpox in the town. The victims could no longer be confined in the old pest-house on the marshland behind the Bear & Key, which had been satisfactory enough when the town was still a street. Instead they were isolated in hospital

Rising Star
Seeshill Farm, Bogshole

1788 Richard Simmens, a yeoman of Bridge, sold to Edward Wacher, a ship-builder of Whitstable, six acres of land at Bogshole called Godly Field. On the death of his son William in 1864 the property which had been built - house, barn and stable - was sold to a farmer Edward Hadlow for £550. The opening of a beerhouse in such a remote spot is traditionally linked with the provision of an isolation 'hospital' for infectious diseases. In early days Whitstable had a 'Pest House' for such sufferers, located on the marsh behind the Bear & Key. When cholera began to spread in 1849 this building had long gone and so fresh provision was made - a room attached to a cottage out at Seasalter. When an epidemic of smallpox began in 1884, probably spread from a ship, some better provision was needed. So as an improvised arrangement a piece of charity land down at Bogshole was rented and three "Piggott's Hospital Tents' were purchased, and a kitchen, wash-house and lavatories were contrived out of two ship's cabins, and two earth closets were constructed. The isolation encampment was looked after by two nurses and a caretaker. At the maximum there were eleven poor souls resident.

After some weeks the camp was cleared in July 1884 only to be reopened in September when a fresh outbreak occurred. This establishment must have been close to the position of the Rising Star. indeed the flint barn next door is still referred to locally as the 'hospital for incurables'. Whether this episode actually started the beerhouse, or whether it was in being and so was able to offer some comfort for the sick and refreshment for those who cared for them, we do not know. Anyway, the public house survived, still owned by the Wacher family until it was sold to Joseph Smith in 1920, and this probably marked its demise. It was said to have been in a very poor condition, largely catering for 'travellers' Today the cottage remains as Seeshill Farmhouse.

tents out at Bogshole, and a new cottage beer-house, the Rising Star, gave some comfort to the sick and refreshed those who ministered to them. Today the building is Seashill farm.

Questions of health and sanitation were soon to become matters of national concern, and they even stirred up a great to-do in Whitstable, as we shall see in Chapter Nine.

Monument
Church Street

The Monument Inn was first licensed in 1731, like several others locally combining a cottage with a forge (in an ancient building opposite by the church). The first licensee was Christopher Figgus (later spelt Figures). The property was owned at the time by William Loathis of Boughton, a grocer, and on his death it passed by family settlement to John Fisher of Canterbury. A later blacksmith tenant, Richard Perkins, purchased both inn and forge. In the later

eighteenth century Canterbury brewer John Cantis became owner and he sold to John Abbott of Thanet. 1825, on his death, it was bought by Rest Flint of the brewery at St. Dunstan's in Canterbury (later Flint & Co). Across the early nineteenth century John & Philadelphia West and later their children were the licensees. Ownership later passed to George Beer of the Star Brewery at Canterbury. Another long tenure was that of John Hayward from 1913 to 1936. The interior was extensively modernised with an open plan in 1981. It is now a Whitbread's 'house'.

7 THE TOWN ALIGHT

For much of its history, Whitstable has consisted largely of shanty structures, mostly made of timber roughly coated with tar to make them waterproof, and roofed often with thatch, all combining to make perfect conditions for large fires.

Fire was a constant hazard. Live embers, ashes carried on the breeze: these were constant dangers. But there's an old saying about familiarity breeding contempt, and people were often reminded to their cost that it took only a strong wind and an absence of any organised fire-fighting apparatus for even a small fire to spread with alarming speed. The close-packed town of the nineteenth century saw a number of serious fires, all of them difficult to

The disastrous fire of 1869.

contain, for fire-fighting expertise was almost non-existent, and all of them caused widespread loss, insurance being a rarity.

Some idea of the speed with which a disastrous fire could strike is found in the events of June 30th 1822. It was a hot Sunday summer's day tempered by a strong wind from the west, a day off work, a day to rest in the shade with the family or to drink a beer or two with the mates, or to mull over the vicar's sermon. Children were listless in the heat, and the sea was dotted with boats, gently rocking in the waves, their halyards slapping against masts.

It was two o'clock. Someone sniffed the air. Surely there was burning. Smoke appeared at the western end of the sea wall. Soon the alarmed folk saw that the thatched roof and wooden walls of a store-shed next to Mr. Gann's house were alight. In minutes the whole shed had gone up. The flames leapt eagerly eastwards, up-wind of dwellings, store-houses, boat houses, a barn and a stable. The inevitable happened: embers carried on the wind meant that the fire took hold with horrifying speed. Soon it had spread to three thatched buildings, full of pitch, paint, and wooden spars. Greedily it took light there, then spread still further to take hold of Mr. Reeve's boat-building workshops below the sea-wall. It spread to more dwelling houses beyond the Duke of Cumberland, some of which were only saved when the line of fire was broken by destroying outhouses. People were beginning to fight now, though the swift spread of the fire was against them. Members of the Royal Navy Blockade Service worked next to men who sometimes defied the blockade, everyone intent on saving what could be saved. Still the fire spread, baulked at times by the hasty knocking down of buildings in its path. By four o'clock, the Kent and Norwich fire engine from Canterbury had arrived, and the immediate danger was over by five. *'The spectacle, however, was that of a scene of smoking ruins towards the sea, from one extremity of the place to the other: while in the street there was scarcely a house on the left side, out of which the furniture was not removed.'*

Altogether nine dwelling-houses, four boat-builder's shops and 33 store-houses were completely destroyed, and many others damaged. Including loss of stock, furniture, clothes, etc., the loss came to what was then the enormous sum of £7,000 of which little more than £1,100 was insured.

In this town that depended so much on oysters, *'the most serious deprivation is that of the poor dredgermen, many of whose boats with their nets and materials were burnt in their different store-houses, so they are absolutely deprived of the means of obtaining a livelihood.'* An appeal for assistance went out: *'The loss unfortunately falls on a class of persons totally unable to bear it and unless the Humane and Charitable afford their assistance, they must be absolutely ruined.'*

No one knew how the fire had started: there was a possibility that sparks from Mr. Gann's chimney had lodged in the thatch of the store-house (but what was he doing with a fire in June?) Then there was a sentence in the newspaper report which carried this information: *'while engaged in endeavouring to arrest the progress of the flames, it was perceived that a storehouse belonging to government on the sea-wall, at the eastern extremity of the place, at least a quarter mile distant from where the fire originated, was also in flames.'* A rogue spark? Or something more sinister? Were the causes of the two fires connected? We shall never know.

In 1854 thatch, tarred wood and wind again contributed to a major disaster when the Zion Chapel, on the site of the present Playhouse, was burnt down. The fire started in a thatched stable, possibly from the ashes of someone's pipe igniting first straw, then hay and 30 tons of coal. Fanned by a strong wind, the fire spread fast: frantically plunging horses in the stable were rescued with difficulty, and three neighbouring wooden houses were soon also ablaze. As usual, fire engines were summoned, for *'There were no appliances for the extinguishing of fires... so when a conflagration took place, we used to have to send to the City of Canterbury for their manual pump which... used to serve the districts for miles around.'* Someone rode so hard for it to be sent, that the horse died, and the rider became known as John Gilpin. In spite of the efforts of this and another engine, it was not long before smoke was seen coming from the roof of the chapel. Frenzied efforts were made to save the house of God, and when the roof was on the point of falling in, *'with utter disregard for his own safety, Mr James Holden dashed into the building and rescued the great bible from the pulpit'*, The fire then leapt across the street and set fire to the roofs of two more buildings, one of them the Queen's Head (now Pirie and Cavenders, booksellers). *'The smoke from the tarred buildings was so dense that it nearly stifled the children in the Endowed School, and they had quickly to be sent home over the adjoining gardens.'* Surely it was time for a local fire engine to be thought of?

Twelve more years passed, before, on the night of Monday 8th October 1866, another great and this time quite unexplained fire swept through the heart of the town. The fishing community of Whitstable was still centred along Harbour Street and the beach by Sea Street, and that part of town still presented a jumble of cottages, taverns, fishermen's stores, sail-lofts and workshops, most (as though no one had learnt a simple lesson) of vulnerable tarred weatherboard and roofing. The fire this time engulfed and destroyed not only the tarred cottages of the poor, but two of the town's ancient inns: the Red Lion and the Duke of Cumberland. Close by, the town's other major hostelry, the Bear & Key, happily escaped.

Again, *'the fire raged and spread with wonderful rapidity. The buildings in which it broke out, being entirely of wood with tarred roofs, were razed to the ground in less than no time so to speak, while the contents, consisting of a large quantity of timber (a stock that had recently been laid in for use in the construction of three houses), coals, tar, rope, and other marine stores, burnt with equal fury... In a very short space of time a crowd of the inhabitants was on the spot to render assistance. With as much speed messengers were dispatched to Canterbury and Faversham for the fire engines, and although*

73

the distance was so great, only two and a half hours elapsed before four had arrived... One and all worked their hardest in endeavouring to extinguish the flames, and to save the surrounding property from destruction.

'The sparks were driven by thousands over a vessel on Mr. Holloway's slipway and shipbuilding premises: the vessel fortunately took no harm, but the thatched roof of the workshop caught fire, and though it was speedily extinguished great apprehensions were entertained for the safety of the Bear & Key, but as it happened the wind was easterly and the stout wall by which the Duke of Cumberland was faced served as a screen to this property against the burning mass.'

This disaster at last concentrated the minds of the townsfolk. There was, surely, urgent need for a local fire-engine: *'Let us hope,'* commented the newspaper, *'the inhabitants will no longer remain indifferent in a matter of such vast importance, but that they will forthwith take the necessary steps to secure for themselves that which for their own safety is so greatly required.'*

A public meeting was called, probably, as was the custom, at the Bear & Key, to 'consider the desirability of the town possessing a fire engine.' Unsurprisingly, no firm decision was reached at the meeting, but seeds had been sown: someone acted on their own initiative and at a second meeting reported that the Norwich Union had offered to provide an engine if a suitable building to house it and the hose could be found.

Once again the meeting was adjourned: the good and careful citizens of Whitstable having decided to approach other insurance companies for help, no doubt hoping for a better deal. So it was not until the July of 1867 that an engine was finally installed - provided by the Norwich Union. Its horses were stabled at the Bear & Key, being usually used to pull the cab to and from the station, and the engine, used until the 1920s, was housed in some old stables behind the Hoy Inn (now the Job Centre). A public appeal was held and 26 men were recruited to be the first members of Whitstable's own fire brigade.

The brigade's first serious test came on the evening of 10th November 1869. On that fateful night, Jacko, a monkey, then resting at his ease in the workshop of a certain Mr. Hoult may have knocked over a candle, roasted himself, and started yet another fire that for sheer intensity more than rivalled that recent one which had burned down the old Duke of Cumberland and The Red Lion, just a step or two down the road.

At about a quarter to eleven a passing coastguardsman noticed flames shooting up from Mr. Hoult's roof. *'He at once raised an alarm, and in a short time a considerable and excited crowd of people had hurried to the spot,*

Victoria Inn
Whitstable Yacht Club, 3 Sea Wall

Details of this building have not been found. The public house is first noted in 1858 with George Foreman as landlord. It was a weather-board building which was rapidly consumed with 71 others in the great fire of November 10th, 1869. The landlord, J. Marsh was insured but the rebuilding was undertaken by one of the breweries. It was on a slightly different site and much larger, indeed it was listed as the Victoria Hotel. By 1900 it had become a Boarding House and in 1903 was purchased by the Yacht Club.

though amid the general confusion little could be done effectually to arrest the progress of the fire, which, as soon as it had burst through the shop-roof rapidly spread to other parts of the building under the aggravating influence of a brisk north-west wind that was blowing.'

As the local paper was again able to report, *'Upon this somewhat straggling site there stood a great number of shanty-looking erections, principally timber, of every variety of design, from a store-house to a rabbit-hutch, and all more or less coated and encrusted with the tar which abounds everywhere thereabouts.'* The fire rapidly took hold and spread to neighbouring buildings.

The crew of the Whitstable fire-engine arrived on the scene with mixed feelings. It looked like being a disaster for the town, but at the same time they would be able to demonstrate their new-found skills to the townsfolk. Surely, they thought, the latest in fire-fighting technology would soon master the flames. So they clanged and clattered their way through the throng of victims, many of them shivering in their night-clothes in the chill air, with high hopes.

But, as the cool eye of the local reporter noted, *'Some time was unavoidably lost in obtaining water and getting the hose into play, and even when this had been accomplished, the work of repressing the momentarily increasing conflagration was after a short time brought to a premature stand-still by the fouling and choking of the engine by the sand and wood drawn up with the sea water from the beach. The flames now had it all their own way, and they devoured the inflammable dry timbered and tarred buildings with a dreadful avidity, which it was next to impossible to withstand. The excitement and the crowds every moment increased, the confusion and distress being heightened by the terrors of the unfortunate people whose dwellings were either being consumed or were in imminent danger of sharing what then threatened to be the common fate.'*

Then into the chaos came Sergeant Walker and his constables. The sergeant, 'with characteristic coolness and energy', took charge, making sure the unfortunate men and women who were fleeing were helped to safety, protecting their property from the hands of looters, and finding fresh sources of water while the town awaited more brigades from Canterbury and Faversham.

But not even they, summoned by telegraph and horseman, could do very much to help the local brigade. The fire was not finally put out till eight o'clock the next morning, and the sad inhabitants, many of them uninsured, could begin to count the cost. A scene of devastation greeted their eyes, the whole area being but a charred ruin. In all 71 buildings were consumed by the flames: 25 houses, 36 stores, sixteen cottages, three sail lofts, a forge, offices, shops, and, last but not least, two taverns: the Victoria and the Spread Eagle. This had truly been the Great Fire of Whitstable.

Shortly after the tragedy the townsfolk came together in a town meeting and an appeal was launched locally and in Canterbury for some 70 persons who had suffered greatly in losing homes, possessions, and livelihood. Attention was drawn to circumstances like those afflicting Widow Walker, who *'had just time to put on her clothes but in her hurry selected her best dress, forgetting that in the pocket of another one was what money she possessed'*, or that of another woman who *'after rescuing her children, who were in their night-dresses, rushed back three times into her burning house to save a few clothes for them... till on the last she emerged from the house with her own dress and the clothes she was carrying all on fire'*. The response to the appeal was generous, over £800 being raised.

No one found out exactly what caused the tragedy. If it was the unfortunate Jacko, then he paid the price: his was the only fatality of that dreadful night.

The fire brigade was completely dependent on the goodwill of local volunteers to man the pumps, and it was not surprising that it could not always answer calls as quickly and efficiently as victims would have liked. There was, for instance, no means of getting news of a fire to the station except by word of mouth. Anyone discovering a fire ran or cycled or rode to the station, and the maroon was fired. Then 'not only did the firemen, all volunteers, hear it, and come a-running but everyone who wanted a cheap thrill joined in'.

Practices were held. A maroon would be fired from the yard of the Bear

Spread Eagle
Christian Meeting House, 10 Harbour Street

On November 10th 1869 a great fire engulfed the eastern
part of Harbour Street and it was at this point that the spread
of flames was finally halted with the destruction of the beer-
house, the Spread Eagle, and the adjacent cottage. The
following day a Captain Jull walked from Sandwich to
survey the smouldering ruins and then stood and preached.
He stayed a few days and his forceful words made a number
of converts and so a small Assembly of Plymouth Brethren
came into being in Whitstable. Although the owner of the
Spread Eagle was insured he did not rebuild and in 1871 he
sold the site to Cephas Foad, a local builder. And here Foad
built a Meeting Room for the Brethren. So, from the ashes
of the fire there arose a House of God, as the history of this
evangelical 'Room' records.

& Key for the Fire brigade to assemble, as far as the members knew for a real
fire. Generally the result was impressive. Within a very few minutes, indeed,
almost before the echoes of the report had died away, from all parts of the town
would be seen men running, hopping along in half a pair of boots, buttoning
tunics, buckling belts, and shouldering their way through the excited crowd.
In the yard of the Bear & Key, horses would be pawing and rearing as they were
taken out of the hotel cab's shafts before being trotted down the road to be
placed between those of the engine. The men lined up, by then almost
completely dressed smartening up in time for the roll-call by Captain Brannon.
Then, at his word of command, the engine, with men a-top, would be pulled,
to the sound of cheers from the assembled crowd, at a spanking pace to the site
of a supposed fire, as it might be the Star Public House, out at Bogs Hole. No
doubt a round of ale was purchased as men eased off tight serge collars, and
shook off their boots before a civilised fire in the grate of the inn and Captain
Brannon praised their swiftness of response. The job was not easy, and
required tough characters, 'none more so than in the days of manual fire
engines when the jets were obtained through sheer back-breaking, exhausting
pumping by muscle and sinew.' Beer was a must therefore, just as important
to the men as money. 'No beer, no water,' or 'More beer' were frequent cries.
Little wonder that practices were popular and the men keen.

So things improved. 'The firemen, engaged upon their day-to-day tasks, or in bed if it were at night, would often be at the station in under a minute, and the engine away in an average of three... a remarkable achievement, for horses had to be brought before the engine could move'. Fires remained common, averaging eighteen a year. Pubs figured in at least three of them.

In 1913 the Steam Packet hard by the harbour gates caught fire, as mentioned earlier, and, being constructed largely of wood, within an hour and a half had burned to the ground. It was early one morning that the landlord heard the falling of glass and the cracking of bottles. He got up and found the bar a mass of flames. As their bedroom was immediately above the bar, there was no time for him, his wife and baby to dress properly. The maid, in her nightgown, ran to the police station, the maroon was fired and within eight minutes the fire brigade was on the spot, hoses attached to hydrants, water being played upon the building. Even though it was only 4.30 in the morning, a large crowd from all parts of the town swiftly gathered. When the fire died down, only the brick-built end walls were standing, and so died a port of call for many a thirsty worker. It was however rebuilt.

Dan Sherrin was a typical Whitstable eccentric, a practical joker and a painter of modest talent who frequently paid his bills by means of his works. He was much admired for his jokes, which were often at the expense of authority, and it was no surprise that the Fire Brigade attracted his wit. Since his house had once caught fire, he was keenly interested in fire engines and for the 1920 carnival he constructed a fire engine float. To accompany this, he printed leaflets, one of which, Fire Form No 1, asked the following questions of people whose property was supposedly afire: presumably it struck a chord with the public.

No 1 State what sort of fire?
No 2 How it happened and what for?
No 3 State if it is near a pub? (Firemen will then hurry a bit)
No 4 State what we shall get for our time and trouble?
No 5 How many in family?
No 6 Married or Single?
No 7 What kind of Beer and whose make kept in house?
No 8 State what quantity of Paraffin kept and if we shall bring any.

Even after fifty years, therefore, the brigade was still the butt of local humour. If anything did convince Whitstable of the value of its fire brigade it was a strange and worrying series of fires in 1932-3. These occurred so

78

regularly on Wednesday evenings that arson was suspected: the Whitstable Times carried a headline 'AGAIN ON WEDNESDAY NIGHT' which headed the report of the worst of these mysterious outbreaks. This, one February evening in 1933, burnt down Spencely's drapery store in the High Street.

Mr. and Mrs. Spencely lived over the shop, as was the custom in those days. On that fateful night they had gone to the cinema. When at eight o'clock smoke was seen issuing from the store, they were brought out of the cinema, and Mr. Spencely's first thought was for his dog, Spot, in the front room upstairs. By then, at a quarter past, the brigade had arrived, and Fireman Webb it was who bravely climbed ladder and brought out the exhausted little dog. *'The worst part of the outbreak was then at the rear of the premises, and the volume of smoke, fanned by a strong north-east wind, soon made the centre of the town appear to be in a dense fog. The cracking of the tiles as the fire spread over the roof at the back of the property, the loud reports as the large plate glass windows were broken as a result of the intense heat, and the fact that it was impossible to turn off the gas at the premises all added to the horror of the conflagration.'* As usual a large and interested crowd gathered at the corner of Gladstone Road, from where the best view was to be had. They saw that it was only with difficulty that the fire was prevented from spreading: Mr Surman, the butcher, who also lived above his premises next door, had many willing hands to carry his furniture across the road to the relative safety of the Salvation Army Hall.

'Be Prepared' now became the watchword of the Fire Brigade. In the following April, when they held their annual dinner at the Marine Hotel - on a Wednesday - two members remained on alert at the Fire Station, and if the maroon had been heard, all was ready, for the fire engine had been prudently parked outside the hotel.

Perhaps it was this preparedness that finally persuaded the people of Whitstable that their old enemy fire had been, if not conquered, at least tamed. What, though, of that other old enemy, the threat of flood?

8 THE FIGHT AGAINST THE SEA

Once again the focus is on the Neptune. Peaceful and placid as the scene around it may be to the summer visitor, natives of Whitstable know that given the right combination of wind and wave the scene can be very different. In the winter of 1853, for instance, *'an unusually high tide with a very strong gale from the north was experienced at this place, doing great damage to a beer house called the 'Old Neptune,' undermining the foundations and rendering it very dangerous. Also washing to pieces an old vessel put there to perform the duties of a break -water.'*

Thirty years later, in 1883, ' a tremendous sea rushed into the bay ,' causing chaos among the craft awaiting or undergoing repair along the shore. A barge, 'Hero,' slipped her moorings, nearly colliding with the 'Hoy Canterbury,' smashing the supports of a slipway upon which rested the 'Kathleen,' and sinking there. The 'Hoy Canterbury' was also driven ashore and her deck cargo only rescued by plucky work in the teeth of a blizzard. In the foul weather Nathaniel Ougham and Onslow Foreman were drowned, last seen through the driving snow, alive and clinging to the keel of their yawl 'Lucy.' Their bodies

Northerly gale batters the 'Old Neptune' - 1938

were later recovered and taken to the Neptune to await the coroner.

The inquest illustrated the way the old pub was becoming a symbol of the town's long and tumultuous relationship with the sea. Every so often in its history it seems that Whitstable needs to be reminded of its dependence upon the waters, and once or twice in every century the elements make a watery onslaught upon the town. The waters rise to a high spring tide, and the wind from a certain quarter sweeps them violently upon the shore.

From Roman times, when the coast was around a mile and a half further out, the sea stole land, and did so unchecked all the time Whitstable was merely a few fishermen's primitive huts. As Whitstable began to grow, walls, made largely of earth and shingle, were built to resist the surges of the sea. Behind the protection of the walls, inns grew up: the Bear & Key and the Duke of Cumberland were among the first surviving today. Some later ones found themselves dangerously near the high water mark, protected by unreliable walls - one, indeed, the Neptune, beyond the safety of any wall. In any case, those primitive structures were none too secure against the biggest storms, frequently giving way, and indeed as late as 1953 no fewer than 2,000 people

81

Old Neptune
Marine Terrace, Island Wall

Originally the beach was much wider than today, so it is not surprising to find a cottage here in 1800, lying outside the recently constructed sea-wall. The owner then, Thomas Richards, sold it and the surrounding 'hard-ground' for £30. By 1844 there were storehouses on either side and the premises were used for boat-repairing with slipways down the beach. Seaward was an old wreck (the Neptune?) which acted as a breakwater. By 1852 a pair of brick cottages had been built on the west side and the cottage was leased by George Beer of Canterbury as a beershop. The first licensee Harry Keam remained for 43 years. Later it was leased by Johnson & Co another city

brewery. Ship building and repairing was now well-established along Island Wall, providing a good trade.

The building was badly damaged in the great storm of 1853 and completely swept away in 1898. The Old Neptune was rebuilt, using much of the material from the ruined cottages by the brewery tenant Tomson & Wotton Ltd, of Ramsgate; they purchased the pub from H.K. Daniels in 1912. The Old Neptune remained unchanged for many years; for 40 years from 1934 the bar was presided over by Mrs Phoebe Ramsley, surviving the battering of the great storms of 1938 and 1953.

Standing out on the foreshore, the inn forms a focal point for the most attractive and frequently painted view at Whitstable. It is now a Whitbread's 'house'.

were made homeless by the town's old enemy undoing the defences yet again.

The Neptune was spared in 1883, but it was not long before the elements again put the old place to severe trial, and with it huge areas of the town. For two dark days in late November 1897, a gale, viewed with knowing suspicion by the townsfolk, had been gathering its strength for a furious onslaught . As at last the wind swung to the north-east it drove the water shorewards, causing another of those monstrous floods that mock the flood defences.

This storm received very extensive coverage in the local papers. The Whitstable Times wrote: *'Here was a town which had been congratulating itself on all sides upon its apparent prosperity, suddenly plunged into the direst depths of distress...there was something ominous in the swirl and impetus of the water that was running , which, to the experienced eye, betokened mischief, but nothing so calamitous as what happened was ever anticipated.'*

High tide, that 29th day of November, was at about four o'clock, but even two hours before that, the waves had broken through the entire length of the sea wall from Tankerton beach to the Salts. At Tankerton it swept through the tea booths, carrying one of them out to sea. The harbour, filled with shipping, found the sea rising above the level of the quays, gushing through the backwater and flooding the land and houses around. Further west it flooded the Salts, lifting and depositing a boat, the 290 ton 'Matilda Calder,' upon them, rising to within a few feet of the old cliff at West Cliff Road, pouring down Nelson Road carrying fences and timber from ship-building yards , flooding the houses to a depth of six feet, filling basements with shingle and other debris , and finally reaching the High Street, where it met in a maelstrom the waters that were pouring down from the direction of the harbour. Business had long before ground to a halt, and shopkeepers, distracted and aghast, were soon viewing seaweed, dead fish, bits of timber and other fruits of the sea swirling about amongst items of soiled stock up to the level of their counters.

Brick-built buildings survived, though with their basements and ground floors filled with rubbish, but many wooden buildings were swept away and destroyed. Among these was the Neptune. As the Whitstable Times reported, *'Perhaps the greatest loss has been the sweeping away of the Old Neptune Inn, kept by Mr. Nat Keam. When the water commenced to rise fears for the safety of the house were entertained...'.* It was with memories of 1853 that Nathaniel Keam began to remove some of the furniture as a precaution. It was as well that he did so, for it was not long before the place had suddenly to be abandoned. Everything remaining inside was lost, and when the tide went down *'all that remained of a house in which many a jovial night has been spent by Whitstable seamen were a few planks.'* The two cottages next to the inn were severely damaged.

The report gives little idea of the horror of those few hours, of the heaving of the rising waters against the old timbers of inn and cottage, of the desperate hope against hope that they would withstand the surge, of the panic removal of furniture through spume and spray, and the despair when the situation was seen to be hopeless by drenched and tired Mr. Keam and neighbours, with the haunting memories of the previous disaster ever present as they watched the sad disintegration once more of the old ale-house.

Damage to property right along the shore was very heavy indeed *'From the site of the Neptune right along to Tankerton severe damage was done, especially to the shipbuilding yards of Messrs. Collar Bros., and Mr. H.C. Solly. At the corner of the Horsebridge Road, the stores, forge and workshops in the occupation respectively of Mr.. Goldfinch and Mr. Foad, were practically non est, while proceeding further along the wall, part of Beach Cottage was seen to be carried away. Mr. Solly's cement store house was missing, and damage done to the oyster store of the Ham and Seasalter Oyster Company. On the east pier the shipbuilding yard of the Whitstable Shipping Company was very much knocked about, and the front of the carpenters' shop was knocked in and the place inundated with water.'*

Elsewhere, distraught parents were searching for children in the storm, and children were found in the street, cold and frightened, crying *'Mother is upstairs and we can't get in because the water is in the house.'*

Surprisingly, no lives were lost, though for one poor old lady it was a close run thing. Mrs. Camburn was 84 years of age, suffering from paralysis, and living alone in a cottage on Middle Wall. 'She was lying on a sofa in the front room, and no-one seems to have thought of her for some time, when Mr. Albert Nutten suddenly remembered her, and with several of his friends rushed to the house and got her out. The sofa on which she was lying was then nearly covered with water.' Another woman, Mrs. Kelcey, aged 66, was found by Captain Foad, who, having heard her crying out for help, found her standing in four feet of water in her own home.

The next day, after the waters had subsided, people began to look around at the devastation. Shopkeepers totted up their losses of swamped and soiled stock. From their shelter in local schools, 100 men and women and 200 children, many of them still wet through and with no change of clothing, began to return in sick anticipation to their flooded homes. Two days afterwards 200 houses still had furniture floating about.

Whitstable rallied round as it had in the past and would in the future. An Inundation Relief Committee was set up, money was collected, initially £1,232 15s 6d locally, good sums from neighbouring towns, and nearly £400 from well-wishers in London. The committee met weekly to distribute the money as needed. Perhaps poor Nathaniel Keam benefitted. He had only had the tenancy of the Neptune for two years, and had invested his own possessions in a bid to make a success of the place. He was not insured against flood, and the cruel sea had almost ruined him.

Yet the Neptune was rebuilt, and, as the town moved into the progressive twentieth century, the fear of floods subsided. Forty years passed.

Then, in 1938, the Neptune was again battered by flood. A high spring tide coincided with a 60 mph northerly wind, and as high tide hit the beach, it came swirling round the building. A nearby breakwater was rammed by a baulk of timber from a shipyard, and gave way. A piece of concrete knocked the bottom out of the Neptune's store-room, the roof of its scullery was washed off, and the water poured in. The outside lavatory was flushed away, and it was only by superhuman efforts that the door at the back was secured enough to save the building from complete inundation.

The Neptune was not alone now. The flood also damaged Pearson's Crab and Oyster House next to the Oyster Stores on the Horsebridge. The publican reported that *'by ten o'clock the water was coming in the front door, and we had it in the bars and the cellar. But the sea wall and the premises of the Oyster Company saved us from being flooded out. We only got the water - not like some people who got the mud and shells and seaweed as well.'* Not to speak of lumps of concrete.

Out at Seasalter, the old farms and new housing and all the low lying land around was under the sea. As one keen motorist wrote: *'One of the most extraordinary experiences I have ever had was my drive home on the Faversham Road, a few minutes after ten o'clock on Saturday night. I rounded the corner past the Blue Anchor with a precision born of past experience and there my well ordered drive finished. I had apparently driven into the sea! To add to this illusion a pair of boots floated towards me. I stopped and surveyed the scene. The road no longer existed. In its place flowed the sea, sweeping on like a mill race, carrying before it wreckage of all descriptions. The huts between the Old Coastguards and the Sportsman were swept together into one solid line where they pounded and ground against each other, tearing off roots and reducing some of the smaller buildings to matchwood. So continuous was the spray that it looked like the playing of hundreds of fire hoses.'* That motorist at least soon got home. Not so the passengers on the last bus from Faversham which was marooned for four hours in the tons of shingle thrown across three hundred yards of the road.

It was clear that something had to be done if the town was not to suffer from anxiety every time the storm clouds gathered and the wind began to build from the North-east. After World War Two, work was put in hand to build concrete walls to replace some wooden breastwork. The work was started in 1951-2, but before it was completed Nature thought to teach the town one further lesson.

The dreadful flood that ensued in 1953 made more than 2,000 people homeless. The Neptune again suffered, as people had known it would, since it stood outside the new concrete wall. Water swept through its bars on its familiar way to town. The Pearson's Arms suffered too as the water built up steadily at the Horsebridge before the waves crashed over the top of the new wall and was funnelled between it and the Oyster Fishery Company's store into the main street. Miss Beryl Waters, licensee, declared *'The first rush came like a tidal wave right over the top of the house. I thought it was the end for me.'* Scores of empty oyster barrels swept away from the Horsebridge were soon bobbing on the water nearly a third of a mile away outside the St. Alphege and Congregational Churches. As far inland as Cromwell Road, one gentleman wrote to relatives that he had found his fireside chair floating up the hall.

Familiar sights emerged: *'the homeless, many without possessions of any kind, some clutching pets and others carrying children wrapped in blankets presented a pathetic sight.'* Voluntary bodies slipped into gear, a reception centre was set up in a school, and householders in higher parts of the town offered temporary accommodation: all those rescued found food and sanctuary. Whitstable was again looking after its own.

That storm, Whitstable's share of the great east coast surge that devastated the coasts of Norfolk, Suffolk and Essex, struck all along the coast between Tankerton and the western end of Seasalter.

Again, the road between the Blue Anchor and the Sportsman, covered deep in shells and shingle, disappeared entirely from view, and nearly all houses and farms in the area were feet deep in water. The sea had torn a 50-foot breach in the sea wall near the Sportsman and with every tide more water was pouring into the Seasalter marshes, fanning out in all directions and forming one unbroken stretch of water as far inland as the Thanet Way, two miles distant. The area had suffered in floods before: in the 1897 inundation, the lower floor of the Sportsman had been flooded and outbuildings smashed.

Now in 1953, another small drama was unfolding there. Mrs Dover, the licensee's wife, was in the last stages of pregnancy. Indeed, she was due to go into the maternity ward at the Kent and Canterbury Hospital the very next day. If it had not been for that, no doubt the couple, used to rough weather, would not have been so concerned. Indeed, they happily slept through the storm until aroused by a loud bumping. The sea was throwing caravans at them. Suddenly made aware of the risk to his wife and their unborn baby, and completely isolated, Mr Dover signalled with a flash lamp until dawn and afterwards with a mirror.

At last a rescue party appeared in a boat and took the couple across to the sea wall. The party then walked and stumbled and clambered over the debris of huts and across breaks in the sea wall, until they reached the Coastguard

Station. Here Mrs Dover lay on a stretcher in a cart and was towed by a tractor that made its way through water and over piles of shingle to a point near the Alberta Cafe, where the road was blocked by a chalet that had been moved bodily by the sea. Working round this last obstacle Mrs. Dover entered a waiting ambulance which took her thankfully to hospital.

Nor was the Tankerton end of town spared. As in previous floods, *'the sea overran the low wall at the top of the beach, surged against the Hotel Continental and nearby cafes and swept along Beach Walk to lick hungrily at the Wynn Ellis Almshouses... The sea front at the end of Beach Walk looked more like a disused battlefield. Shingle covered the road to a depth of over a foot.'*

Through the years, the sea had other tricks up its sleeve, in the shape of what the newspaper called 'King Frost'. In 1877, indeed, a fishing smack was sunk, and others were nearly lost by having their sides scraped away at the water line by ice. Brigantines were driven by wind and ice out of the harbour and into the bay: 'it was with the greatest difficulty that they were got back'. Again, in 1929, the sea froze over, and some fishermen, due back at 6.30 am, were finally got back by a rescue party at 4 pm, more dead than alive, frozen, and with ambulances and oxygen awaiting them. In 1963, frozen waves piled up on the beach around the Neptune as the sea froze along the entire six miles of coastline. Looking out of the one window which faced seawards, its patrons could see the pack ice extending out for nearly a quarter of a mile, while the temperature dropped to eighteen degrees Fahrenheit. Inland, cars crashed, forty people were taken to Kent and Canterbury Hospital with fractures of arms and legs, old people went done with pneumonia and flu, electric power was lost from time to time, and there was a big rush on oil heaters, fur-lined boots, warm clothing - and also quite a lot of swimsuits: in prudent preparation, no doubt, for better times ahead.

It is doubtful that suspicion of the sea will ever be removed from the minds of Whitstable people. Frosts are one thing, floods quite another. The present state-of-the-art sea-defences are based on a newly constructed beach whose steep seaward face is designed to break the waves before they reach the sea wall. But even this would not be proof against the sort of storm that must, according to statisticians, hit Whitstable once in every thousand years or so. Till that dreadful day, if it ever comes, the town will cherish the Neptune, a lasting symbol of the town's defiance.

9 THE BEAR & KEY

In 1849 the people of Whitstable were split down the middle, and all because some outsiders had organised a petition that criticised their cleanliness.

To the fresh eyes (and noses) of outsiders, there was some cause for alarm. In 1834, 65 people had died of cholera, and only two years previously, in 1847, four people had died in Church Street of typhus. The local vicar, the Rev Morris, new to the town and worried for his flock, was one of those who had signed the petition sent in 1848 by concerned ratepayers to the new government body, the General Board of Health. In a covering letter he had written *'the people have been so long enured to the habits of filthiness that it is most difficult to arouse them to a sense of their danger, and to the necessity of removing all nuisances that engender disease.'* He little knew what a hornets' nest he had stirred up around his own ears, for he was ignorant of the town's abiding satisfaction with things as they were.

Rising proudly above the insanitary conditions and potential disease, its patrons ignoring privies empying into open drains and children dying of cholera, was the Bear & Key Hotel. Its grandeur and imposing appearance, rather out of place in the little town, together with its 250 years of history, managed to give its wealthy customers a sense of serene unshakeable security. In contrast to the homes of most of the people of Whitstable, which were no more than simple weatherboard cottages, its two grand storeys with attics above had long been the scene of august celebrations, the centre of polite society. It was always chosen as the venue for major celebrations, formal meetings and secret gatherings: the ancient Manorial Courts, the Court Leet and Court Baron, met within its walls. The essential feature of the gatherings was dinner, and until 1896, the Brannans, father and son, maintained an outstanding reputation for sumptuous repasts, followed, 'when the cloth was removed' by speeches, music, songs and general conviviality.

In May 1849 there was an influential guest: Mr. T.W. Rammell, the government's Board of Health Inspector. He was making the first of two visits to Whitstable in response to the petition. His brief was clear: he was to enquire into 'the Sewage Drainage, and Supply of Water and the Sanitary Conditions of the inhabitants of the Town of Whitstable.' It was to the Bear & Key that he called his witnesses, and from the Bear & Key that he made his forays into the town to see conditions for himself.

His investigations stirred up so much mud as to raise a stink of enormous proportions. The tone was set in a preliminary letter he sent to the General Board of Health: *'The town has literally no drainage and it may be described without exaggeration as squatted in its own filth.'* It was this sort of remark that was to make the Bear & Key the centre for bitter argument and recrimination. In the part in his full report about sewage disposal, if such it could be called, he stated that he had found one sewer *'along the east side of the town, and one other, half filled with deposit, that ran along the main street'*, and to which the Bear & Key probably had access.

But so did others... As Widow Beal said, the *'drain from the street passes under my wash-house, and nothing to cover it except a few planks; the smell from it, in certain states of the weather, is exceedingly bad... After the heavy rains, the wash-house and sitting rooms were completely flooded; the smell from the water was very bad; we suffered afterwards from colds... 14 pailfuls of filthy water were taken from the rooms.'*

But Mr. Rammell found that most people did not have access even to such an inadequate sewer as this. Many of them relied on their own resources and built privies above or on the side of ditches. They were, Mr. Rammell wrote, *'in most cases a slight wooden erection completely detached from the house, often without a door, and at its base on the ditch side a large heap of excrement usually is to be seen.'* Sometimes the people used tubs or boxes underneath their privies. These were *'adopted chiefly by the seafaring population living along the shore; their contents are usually discharged into the sea, into a ditch or into a stagnant pool, of which there are several along the beach.'* The smell from the beach was insufferable. Or there were vaults sunk under the privies, *'very small in size, and half or three fourths filled with land water; and when they become completely filled with faecal refuse, the common practice is to withdraw the solid portion of this matter and cast it into the nearest ditch; some times it is buried, but very seldom; sometimes it is carried away.'* One resident, Mr. James Wood, said, *'I have a vault to the privy of my own house; when it is full I take the matter into my own yard, and mix it with coal ashes.'*

As this sort of thing had been going on for centuries, it is no surprise to find that the wealthier, older-established rate-payers had become so accustomed to the filth and disease around them that they were totally opposed to any increase in the rates to improve things.

Then there was the matter of clean water. There should have been no problem, for Whitstable was blessed by the presence of clean water 60 or 70 feet beneath ground, water that merely had to be tapped. It was easy enough: a pit had to be dug about four feet across and eight feet deep, then a 2½ inch augur used to bore a hole through the clay down to the water. This then rose up to within two feet of ground level. Many people sank their own wells: there is one to be seen today in the Bear & Key itself.

On the face of it, there seemed to be no problem with water. But, *'The great number of the wells are kept in a most slovenly manner, very commonly without any cover, and with a pool of filthy water stagnating near their mouths, and at times dripping into them... the water in nearly all of the wells in the town is more or less polluted.'* Taken all round it is hardly surprising to find Mr. Auld, the headmaster of the charity school, writing: *'The children attending the school are by no means healthy looking, they are pale, and there is a good deal of ague amongst them; there is more absence from the school on account of ill-health, than from any other cause.'*

Nor was that all, for the keen eye of Inspector Rammell had also noted a complete lack of public lighting in the fair-sized town.

The inhabitants of Whitstable were incensed with Rammell's report, they believed with some justification. They pointed out the undoubted beneficial effects of good clean sea air, and said that other Kentish towns had a death rate considerably higher than theirs. They emphasised with pride the longevity of their inhabitants: *'There are now living within the district upwards of 239 persons whose average age exceeds 75 years, several of whom do regular daily labour.'* So, far from rousing the inhabitants to a recognition of danger, and far from encouraging the majority of ratepayers to do anything about the situation, the report caused fury, and split the town. The division was essentially between established families and newcomers to the district. Within a month a public meeting was held in the field behind the Bear & Key, at which five-sixths of the ratepayers of the town raised objections to the report. A 'memorial' was sent to the authorities, expressing alarm at the contents of Rammell's report, claiming that much of the evidence given to him had been exaggerated, and saying that the original petition to central government had been rigged - 'got up in an improper manner' - and signed by people in 'total ignorance of its object.'

Clearly, most of the ratepayers were set against anyone who dared to expose the town's unhygienic ways. As tempers rose, no trick was too low to be used by worthy citizens opposed to any clean-up of 'their' town. Soon they were waging covert warfare on those newcomers who had caused the unwelcome descent of 'the man from the ministry', and by March 1850, they were able to send off an even more defiant memorial. This stated that *nearly every inhabitant was opposed to the scheme to set up a local board of health, and that it had been determined to use every legal means to prevent the compulsory measures of the act to be carried out.'* By now a good many of the original signatories were saying they were now bitterly sorry to have signed the petition, and wished to withdraw their names.

Mr. Rammell came back to the Bear & Key to delve into the accusations of rigging, and satisfy himself that everything was above-board. He therefore approached the poor Rev. Morris and a Mr. Williams, asking them to act as Chairman and Vice-chairman of a meeting to set up a local board of health. But by now they were scarred and battle weary. Mr. Morris's reply to Mr. Rammell testified: *'I am as convinced as ever of an Act to improve the sanitary condition of the town, but I cannot consistently with my spiritual duties sacrifice my position as their minister. No sooner did your first report appear than several persons immediately absented themselves from Church to which they have now returned, and in the wake of the Provisional Order on Saturday last our service on the following Sunday was most lamentably interfered with. Many, very many persons would not come at all, others came, and walked out again as soon as the service commenced, and if I were to insist upon taking the Chairmanship I have no doubt that the Church would be completely deserted.'* He went on to write of the awful prejudice he had faced from the people, who were *'proof against all reason and argument.'* The coarse vilification and threats he had received had broken him down *'in mind and body'*. Similarly, Mr. Williams stated that he had himself *'suffered a martyrdom already,'* and was not looking for another.

The delaying tactics worked: it was not until well into the twentieth century the patrons of the Bear & Key, and Whitstable people in general, were able to enjoy proper sanitation.

By then the Bear & Key was more than 200 years old. It had been advertised in Victorian times as 'established in 1703', but in fact deeds can be

Town Map Detail 1725

The Ship

Bear & Key
Commercial Inn
1850

years the Hockless family were licensees. In 1761 the inn was purchased by John Cantis, brewer of Canterbury and he sold to John Abbott of Thanet in 1785. In the later eighteenth century the old inn was rebuilt with a grand Georgian facade. It offered accomodation to passengers travelling to and from London by hoy, a hostelry for wealthy local people, and facilities for the new fashion of sea-bathing.

New facade and additional floor 1870

By the nineteenth century the Bear & Key was Whitstable's premier establishment, now owned by Flint's of Canterbury. Under the management of the Brannons it had a great reputation for fine wines and splendid food.

Around the 1870s the present massive facade was built, the hotel having extensive accomodation and public rooms. After World War One it became either privately owned or part of a Company Group. Today the building still dominates the Cross, the centre of Old Whitstable, and is a very potent reminder of more affluent days

Bear & Key (Ship)
High Street

Property deeds in the name of Edward Basset, date back to 1604; the property later passing to the Spencer and then the Pembroke families. The inn at 'The Sign of the Ship', indeed the 'new Ship', as there was an old one also for some years, was established in 1703. The first licensee noted was John Hampton the next year. In 1739 a new tenant from Canterbury, William Hogsflesh, changed the sign to the Bear & Key. 1746 and for many

traced back to 1604 when Edward Bassett owned the property. The town map of 1720 clearly shows this 'Ship' as a single-storey building, probably only a humble tavern catering for local fishermen and sailors. In 1739 a new licensee William Hogsflesh changed the name to the Bear Key and then gave it the following year as the Bear & Key.

This new name reflected the growing link with London. Daniel Defoe, writing in 1724, referred to 'the Bear key, one of the two great corn markets in the City of London' to which came 'all the vast quantity of corn that is brought into the city by sea.' Corn and hops were major exports of East Kent, and they flowed through Whitstable to London. In 1761 when Whitstable was enjoying a growth spurt with more wealthy inhabitants and more passengers passing through on their way to London by hoy, the inn was bought by John cantis, a brewer in Thanet. He was probably responsible for rebuilding the old inn and giving it a richly handsome Georgian facade.

It became the focus for what might have become a thriving seaside town. Elsewhere, sea bathing was fast becoming the fashion, and efforts were made to promote it in Whitstable, especially by Elizabeth Hockless of the Bear & Key. In 1798 she advertised in the Kentish Gazette. Two essentials for visitors were available: the first was the provision of bathing machines, essential for discreet entry into the water: *'Now in full perfection are ready for reception of Ladies and Gentleman.'* The second was a place to stay: *'Good accommodations, with the best of wines, etc.'* She added *'NB Private Lodging, to be had very genteel and readily furnished. A good Turnpike-road from Whitstable to Canterbury.'*

A later advertisement for the Bear & Key drew attention to the attraction of Whitstable: *'There is exceeding agreeable Prospect both of Sea and Land,'* it said, but was careful not to draw attention to the town itself. Still later, landlord Stephen Perkins vigorously promoted the Bear & Key, *'where he has laid in a good assortment of Wines and all liquors of the best sorts,'* and further, *'He has likewise erected A NEW BATHING MACHINE on the newest and most approved Principle: Where Ladies and Gentlemen will be properly accommodated with careful Guide and Driver and their commands most thankfully acknowledged. There is good Bathing in Whitstable Bay near Six Hours every Tide'*. To encourage day visitors in 1792 was the advertisement: *'A Light Coach and Pair, from the Bear & Key in Whitstable to the King's Arms in St. Peter's Street, Canterbury, every day in the week during the summer season.'*

But the older inhabitants of Whitstable, unsurprisingly, continued to see the town solely as a place of work, and not as a burgeoning seaside resort like its neighbour Herne Bay. Even the eulogy published in the 'Railway Companion' of 1836 in an effort to drum up passenger travel on the new railway failed to have any great effect. *'In the whole range of marine summer resorts,'* it puffed enthusiastically, *'there is no spot offering so many inducements to the speculator. The inland scenery is commanding; the beach for sea-bathing excellent; the air remarkably pure; the water good and abundant.'*

And this only two years after 65 people had died of cholera in the town.

The lack of local interest in providing amenities and suitable accommodation for visitors was constant through the nineteenth century, as is evidenced by this from the 'Companion', where a truth peers shyly through: *'It is not too much to anticipate (if Whitstable were provided with good lodging houses and commodious Inns) that in a short time, it would become a place of fashionable resort.'* Nevertheless the Bear & Key did get a special write-up in the journal. Here was to be found, it stated, a *'Catch and Glee Club, Assisted by an orchestra, respectably conducted by native talent.'* This met weekly through the winter months and *'is supported by the principal inhabitants of the place; and not infrequently numerous visitors from Canterbury and elsewhere, contribute to enliven the harmony of the evening.'* There was clearly some culture in the town - as well as cholera.

But evening meetings at the Bear & Key were probably difficult, except on moonlit nights, for as Rammell had reported, there was no street lighting. At the defiant meetings that had met his report, the usual sort of cry had gone up. Moonlight had been good enough for their forefathers, why change? Besides, where was the money to come from? It quickly came in fact from private enterprise. A company was formed, shares were issued, and work went ahead so rapidly on building a small gas-producing plant near the harbour that gas-lighting was inaugurated in the very September of the year of the enquiry, 1850. The whole town turned out to witness the occasion, and the Kent Gazette reported on the one lamp in somewhat exaggerated terms: *'The town is now lighted with gas. On the first evening the shareholders and consumers, with several gentlemen from the neighbouring towns dined together at the Bear & Key Inn. Not less than 3000 people were assembled to witness the illumination in front of the inn, and the setting off of fire balloons.'*

Individual public buildings were soon illuminated: the Wesleyan Chapel in November, and, not to be outshone, St. Alphege in the following February. The installation of lighting in the harbour was actively considered: accidents such as falling in the harbour when intoxicated were not unknown. Within a year most of the High Street traders had laid on gas, and the number of consumers had reached 70. But public provision of street lighting was slow, for public provision meant public funds. It was not till December 1865, indeed, that the first publicly provided street light was lit at The Cross outside the Bear & Key. Indeed, until well into the twentieth century, it was the massive decorative gas lamps outside the principal shops were the main source of lighting for the public, and it was fifty years or more before the town could truly be said to be 'lighted with gas'.

The Bear & Key continued to prosper as the town crept towards the twentieth century. Perhaps it was even getting a little smug. There is an old inn sign of the Bear & Key in The Castle, and on it the bear is seen to have a very smug expression as he hugs to his bosom a large key. The story goes that the young bear married, but failed to give up his bachelor ways, arriving home late each evening, sometimes the worse for wear. His wife, a spirited lady, took against such behaviour by locking him out each night and showering his with missiles, (hence the saying a bear with a sore head?) The bear eventually sought the help of a cunning locksmith who wrought him a master key, so that he was then able to come and go as he pleased. Hence the smug expression.

Be that as it may, the place was doing well. Guests from out of town reported: *'We put up at the Bear & Key which we find a thoroughly comfortable hotel, where attention and economy of charges are co-existent. Having digested dinner, we take a stroll... Whilst enjoying our pipes in the evening several inhabitants of the town drop in to the commercial room, but their manners are far more congenial and social than those of most Englishmen who at the outside can utter but some dull platitude as to the weather when they meet a stranger. The result was that a pleasant evening was spent, the remembrance of which will not soon be forgotten,.'* As if to prove that it was indeed Whitstable they were visiting, the piece in a Gravesend paper concludes, *'Oysters was a good topic of conversation.'*

By that time, the days of interesting medieval relics such as open privies were fast passing. Courts Leet and Courts Baron, too, were now mere formalities, and the Bear & Key found itself the centre instead of the ways of democracy. On March 20th 1880 a meeting of Conservative electors was held there to prepare for the forthcoming election.

In succeeding weeks, the town resounded to the drums and fifes of local bands, and the strident tones of rival Liberal and Conservative candidates. The Bear & Key and the Music Hall nearby were crammed with rival supporters, for *'the exciting event of an election was sufficient even to stir this little town into some show of enthusiasm and eager interest...'.*

As is common, claims and counter-claims were made, and the debate became increasingly noisy and bad-tempered. So much so that the local vicar, the Rev Blissard, wrote to the local paper, as though thundering from his pulpit: *'I desire in particular to enter a serious protest those electioneering Popes, who at a time when judgement has to be formed on circumstances of singular complexity, denounce those who differ from them, as though wanting in righteousness, humanity and wisdom. A General Election is unhappily a carnival too much of passion and prejudice, and they serve their country best who in a season of national excitement remain fair-minded and charitable.'*

Alas, poor Mr. Blissard, passions remained high, ending on election evening with an immense crowd *'spending some of their surplus energy in fighting, and throwing flour, rotten-eggs, etc., which did no further damage than breaking a few windows.'* A few old scores were no doubt light-heartedly settled, as in the case of the *'well-known and highly respected barber'* who was *'plentifully smothered in soot by some indiscriminating individual.'*

The Conservatives just scraped home with 206 votes against 201 for the Liberals and at the Bear & Key the committee held a celebration oyster supper for the victorious candidates before joining with 170 of their supporters in the large room: *'The remainder of the evening was spent in conviviality.'*

Conviviality! That word sums up the Bear & Key at that time. For 50 years of the nineteenth century its reputation for good food, fine wines and convivial company was immense. A typical report described how *'A menu calculated to excite the imagination of the most fastidious epicure was ably served by the indefatigable proprietor, Mr. W. Brannon.'*

In 1896, Mr Brannon the younger retired. Change was afoot. Soon the old queen would die, and with her the Victorian age. As if in sympathy, fewer sailing ships crowded the harbour and anchored in the bay, and the old organisation of the oyster industry based on the association of Freemen also gave way, replaced by a modern share-holding company. The 1890s, too, saw the auctioning of farmland around the old town for building plots: eventually sprawling estates would surround and submerge the old town centre. With all this change the prestigious reputation of the Bear & Key faded too. After the First World War it was to the Marine Hotel, in the 'new town' of Tankerton, that society repaired for dinner and dancing. So it is that the hostelry which had seen much of the town's history, which had watched the town grow from a few fishermens' huts to a thriving nineteenth-century maritime town remains a symbol of times gone by, of Whitstable in the convivial age of Victoria.

10 A PLACE FOR WEALTH & HEALTH

Marine Parade, Tankerton, is an esplanade with a splendid panorama of the sea from the long greensward of the slopes. Half-way along it there is the Marine Hotel, its gables and woodwork dating from Edwardian days when the better-off took their holidays at the English seaside. But a close look at it shows evidence of four separate entrances: clearly this was built as a terrace of separate houses. Here, then, is a little history to unravel, and it can be launched with a bottle or two of champagne.

Herr Mohr was a man who liked his wine and his 'stein', a man on the look-out for a jolly life. So when he met an Englishman in London named Hudson who was pally and invited him to enjoy a little run to a little seaside town called

Taking the air on Tankerton Slopes.

Whitstable, the German readily agreed, particularly as his new-found pal had not only a railway ticket for him, but a free ticket for a lunch with all the trimmings.

Arrived in Whitstable, it seemed that Hudson knew his way around, for their first port of call (and indeed their only port of call) was to a lunch in a special saleroom.

This was in a converted building, the old Tan Barn on the north side of present-day Kingsdown Park. Its mud floor cemented, windows and doors installed, a galvanised-iron extension constructed, festooned with bunting of various colours, the place was very jolly, humming with noisy conversation amid the clatter of cutlery and the clink of glasses.

Herr Mohr was enchanted, and readily mixed with the couple of hundred guests who were presented with a most sumptuous luncheon provided by Mr. Brannon of the Bear & Key: *'the menu was a liberal one, the viands were of the best, and the wines of the choicest'*. Crowded though it was, Herr Mohr noticed that his new friend Hudson was never far from his side. *'An excellent lunch,'* he confided to him, and Hudson smilingly agreed: beer and ham,

Marine Hotel
Marine Parade, Tankerton

The facade of the hotel readily shows that this was built as a terrace block of four large houses. Cliff Terrace was indeed built as a prestige development by the Tankerton Estate Company, to set the standard for the grand resort they had planned. It was completed in 1895 in the popular Queen Anne style; the architect was one of the Company Directors Basil Champneys. Mr George Fitt Senior converted the eastern pair of houses into an hotel in 1906. During the First World War the whole block became a military hospital. Then in 1919 when the hotel section was restored the other half continued until 1921 as Whitstable's first hospital. Mr Fitt then bought the whole block and in 1926 the fully established Marine Hotel was opened. Before the Second World War the hotel was patronised by visitors both winter and summer, and it became the local venue for dances and banquets. In recent years it has suffered something of a decline from its heyday, but refurbishment will doubtless restore its reputation. The Marine is owned by Shepherd Neame.

champagne and cold beef were part of a coldly conceived plan that would leave Herr Mohr the poorer and himself the richer. He busied himself in making sure that the innocent German's glass was never empty, and soon the gay colours, the hubbub, and the half-heard speeches combined with the liquor to produce a not-unexpected stupor in the man.

Later, in the County Court in Edmonton, London, when sued for his deposit money, the German said that he believed that some time in the afternoon he signed a paper, but could not remember what it was about. Pressed further, he said he could not even remember what time he got on the train to come back to London, alone. Hudson, another defendant in the case, was asked what sort of man Herr Mohr was. 'He always uses saloon bars,' was the reply, and there was knowing English laughter in the court. Asked why he gave the tickets to the German, he replied, boldly, that it was because he thought him a likely customer The judge found for the defendants, and severely criticised this method of conducting an auction sale.

What was it that was being sold with such vigour, with no expense spared, and with underhand methods not entirely frowned upon?

It was the close of the nineteenth century, and when Herr Mohr visited, Whitstable was in the early stages of a kind of fever. It was a fever brought on by the continuing growth of London, and the desire of many people to move out to a peaceful little place in the country, preferably within sight of the sea. It was an innocent dream that big business set out to satisfy.

In 1891, a syndicate of out-of-town businessmen bought up Grimsgill Farm, an ancient medieval estate. This almost surrounded Borstal Hill with its rustic Windmill, and lay along the Canterbury Road south of the railway station and up the steep slope to the edge of Clapham Hill. As the local paper reported, *'From its heights most extensive and magnificent views of the sea are obtained.'*

'Freehold land for the People' ran a typical advertisement, with all the blandishments of the modern adman. A plot 20' by 150' for only £5; the first payment 10/- and the balance paid in nine quarterly payments, *'which means only putting by in the savings box or Post Office Savings Bank a little over 9d a week!'* For this first sale in the May of 1891, the pattern was set: free travel by special train from London, transport to the site and a free luncheon in a marque. Mr. Brannon of the Bear & Key, who seems to have profited mightily in the atmosphere of land fever, was asked to prepare a luncheon for 300 guests, and the town band was engaged to play a selection of music *'while the party are discussing the viands provided for their entertainment.'* In fact the catering ran out, to Mr. Brannon's mortification, for 600 people attended. Feasted or not, the crowd was in a hearty and relaxed mood by auction time. 170 plots were sold at prices ranging from £5 to £50.

Nine more such Sales followed: by October no less than 1,800 plots had been taken.

The fever spread. In the following year, another ancient farm, Rayham, succumbed, closely followed by the Martins Down estate. In came the special trains (now making a slight charge, refundable on purchase of a plot), but luncheon remained free, and sales boomed.

There was very little in the way of overall amenity planning: what nowadays would be called 'infrastructure' was noticeable by its absence: occasional plots were set aside for shops or hotel, but most were for dwellings, and a picture emerged of *'undulating lands adjacent to the Town being rapidly dotted over with the modest dwellings of successful industry, and the more pretentious abodes of retiring wealth',* in which either class could now possess *'a tranquil cot in a pleasant spot, with a distant view of the changing sea.'* For many that vision was all that remained, an idyll to be taken up at later date; for others the whole affair was harsh reality as they woke up and wondered, with Herr Mohr, why and how they had become the owner of a tiny plot of land far from home down the line at Whitstable. But owners they had become, all signed, sealed and delivered.

The engineers of change also had designs on the windy open farmland and the unspoilt bay at Tankerton, and it was at an auction here that Herr Mohr had spent his day. For long the area had been protected from development by the Lord of the Manor, but in 1890, he sold his title and his estate for £16,000 to a London barrister and entrepreneur who then formed the Tankerton Estate Company which bought all the land north and east of the railway lines for £23,000; a handsome profit. The whole development was planned to be rather grander than the piecemeal exploitation that was going on elsewhere. No expense was to be spared as the company announced *'the complete development of this magnificent Property as a new seaside Watering Place of the first class.'* Mr. A. A. Kemp was appointed Clerk of Works. As a man of great energy and talent, it was he who took the rough layout sketched by the directors of the Company and turned it into a detailed scheme for what was hoped to be

---

Royal (Pavilion)
Marine Parade, Tankerton

This single storey building with its bars opened in 1894 as the Pavilion, the permanent sale-room of the Estate Company which began its development of the area in 1890. Potential purchasers were lured down to Whitstable by special train and given a splendid luncheon here; no expense was spared to induce a relaxed state of mind in which bids were made and contracts signed. In 1899 the hotel block was added with 35 rooms at a cost of £20,000. The original section continued as the Pier Pavilion with summer concerts and banquets as well as the auction sales. During the First World War together with a number of properties along the Marine Parade it became a military hospital. Then as St. John's Hospital it continued from 1921 to 1926 as Whitstable's local hospital, which had been first established at the Marine in 1919. In 1926 the present Cottage Hospital was opened. In 1935 the Royal Hotel was extensively refurbished and it flourished until the war years. More recently, with the decline of Tankerton as a seaside resort the hotel has been converted to flats leaving the bars occupying the original building. The Royal is a 'free house'.

a little Eastbourne on the north coast of Kent.

But it was not to be, though not for want of trying. To encourage potential buyers, the company set about building one or two prestige properties in a key position. But it was slow going: a recession had set in and bankruptcies were becoming common in the building trade, so that it was not until 1895 that those four double-fronted houses known as Cliff Terrace were completed. Each had a pleasant basement and no less than seventeen rooms, and all were destined one day to be united as the Marine Hotel.

A detached house next door, Homestead, was sold in 1896 for £1250 and became a House of Rest, so beginning a trend that set the character of the new development for years to come, in which the bracing air of Tankerton was exploited as a 'tonic' for the frail, elderly, and sick. (The injured too came later).

It was also around this time that a pioneering Home for the Aged was founded in Tankerton: well before its time, and setting a trend ultimately responsible for Marine Parade's present-day nickname: Costa Geriatrica.

Meanwhile, sales of plots went on. The Tan Barn was demolished and a new purpose-built sale room was put up at the end of what was to become Pier Avenue: it was 'of a fairly ornamental character', having kitchen and bedroom accommodation, and was designed to seat 150 people at a sale. Again, excellent cold collations were provided by the redoubtable Mr. Brannon for the railway passengers from London. At first the refreshment was free, but the company was over-reaching itself, and it was not long before recession forced the company to make a small charge. Further financial pressures forced them to lease the place to a well-known caterer, Mr. Offredi, as a restaurant known as The Pavilion. Like the Marine, it too had an interesting history before emerging as today's Royal.

Development in Tankerton was slow. The Town Council reluctantly took over responsibility for the cliffs and beach frontage and it was not till the end of the decade that all of Cliff Terrace was occupied. However, a few plots were being developed and the rectangular ground plan of 'little Eastbourne' was gradually coming into reality.

The slow development, unwelcome as it must have been to investors, somehow added charm to the place, and, indeed, may have set a pattern still discernible today. At any rate, in 1901, a 'New Resident' was moved to write to the Whitstable Times: *When one has been to uncomfortably crowded seaside spots in nearly every coast in England, it is possible to recognise the latent attractions of such a natural paradise as Tankerton. Up from the busy harbour of Whitstable, where close, narrow streets dominate, one wanders past the Tower with its open grounds at present bursting with spring verdure, only too eager to display its beauties, to a hill overlooking Tankerton itself, as yet in embryo. Dotted here and there are newly built houses, a few only occupied. Looking back is the charming sea view of a whole flotilla of tugs, fishing and oyster boats, seaward is a vast expanse of ocean as grand as any Kent town could boast.'* In order to realise the potential of this 'paradise' the writer continued: *'Enterprise must take a place in the foreground. Afternoon concerts should be promoted, evening plays with a talent of good order should be provided; a suitable pier should be built, and shelters erected along the beautiful parade. We, who are new residents, firmly believe that with a few improvements Whitstable-cum-Tankerton will become one of the most popular and charming health resorts in the country.'*

When he wrote, Cliff Terrace consisted of a Convalescent Home run by the London Hospital, two boarding houses, and the St. Vincent's Industrial Home for orphan boys. Ten years later, the 'paradise' was emerging. By then,

Tankerton Arms (Hotel)
Marine Parade, Tankerton

The development of Tankerton by the Estate Company commenced in 1890. Initially they aimed at a high quality resort: a sort of little Eastbourne. Along the Marine Parade grand buildings were envisaged and one of the few that was built was the Tankerton Hotel. Opened in 1902 by Mackesons of Hythe it cost £10,000 and was intended to "excel the County of Canterbury". In the early days it flourished and was extended with an additional wing in 1912. The grass area opposite belongs to the property and here on the 'Lawn' summer concert parties performed - most notably the Jollity Boys - eventually there was a covered stage and a fenced inclosure with a little ticket kiosk. After the Second World War the demand for accommodation declined and the hotel rooms were converted into flats and eventually the restaurant closed, leaving just the bars. So it has been appropriately renamed the Tankerton Arms; it is a 'free house'.

St. Vincents had moved to a new building beside the Catholic Church and in 1906 the end two houses of Cliff Terrace became the Marine Hotel, proprietor, Mr. George J. Fitt. Further along Marine parade towards the Castle, the Tankerton Hotel had opened in 1902, built by Mackeson's the brewers at a cost of £10,000 to 'excel the County Hotel in Canterbury'. Boarding houses catered for holidaymakers, while the council saw that the rough grass along the cliff tops was tamed, and provided some seats, a shelter, and a bandstand. At the foot of the cliffs a line of beach huts appeared - little homes in which people could spend, if they wished, days and even nights in companionable comfort Across the road from the Tankerton Hotel the Jollity Boys presented summer shows. Towards the old town, the tea-booths at the end of Beach Walk were improved; a couple of restaurants appeared, and nearby at Cosy Corner pierrots appeared in the summer months. There were cinemas, boat-rides, a rink for roller-skating, and always the sight of boats and ships in the busy harbour. And there were always the older and more traditional pubs. For many, a little paradise indeed.

But earthly paradises don't last. On the evening of August 1914, at pubs like the Neptune, a quiet evening was being spent more than usually soberly, for war had that very day been declared. At the cinema a timely film 'The Curse of War' was being shown: on the screen, an airship was about to blow up. Suddenly, somewhere outside, a heavy explosion rent the air. The Neptune suffered a broken window, and cinema-goers, disoriented by the news, the noise and the picture before them, left in panic. Speculation, rumour and general agitation took over the town.

The explosion was found to be the result of an accident at Faversham Gunpowder Works. Mr. Pink, the landlord of the Duke of Cumberland, decided to drive over to view the devastation. He was accompanied by Carmelo, an Italian chauffeur. Stopped on the way they were promptly arrested as spies, suspicions being particularly aroused by Carmelo's broken English. War had come with a bang to waken the sleepy town. Reserves were called up, kit-bags packed, pub regulars and others disappeared, horses were commandeered, visitors packed buckets and spades and left for home, there was a run on food supplies, armed coastguards patrolled the beaches, and out at sea could be seen the searchlights of a great cruiser fleet.

The Admiralty commandeered the Convalescent Home at No. 1 Cliff Terrace, the resident patients returned to London, and Tankerton, bracing Tankerton, came into its own as a refuge for the sick and injured. Local ladies organised themselves into a branch of Queen Mary's Needlework Guild to provide suitable items for wounded men: striped flannel shirts, red flannel nightingales, covers for hot-water bottles, blankets and sheets. The good ladies had not long to wait. In October a large party of wounded Belgian soldiers arrived in Canterbury, and ten of them were assigned to Tankerton. 'Many persons followed the wagon to the Convalescent Home to see the *wounded soldiers enter the Home, where, with the skilled attention that they will receive, helped by the bracing climate of Tankerton, they will undoubtedly make a speedy recovery.'*

The trenches of Flanders seemed then to be not so far away. All over town soldiers were billeted, recruitment drives were held, the names of volunteers were published in the local paper; a strict blackout was enforced to foil Zeppelins; the beach huts were demolished and two trenches ran along the top of the cliffs; while the weekly casualty lists too often showed how local men were making 'the final sacrifice'.

And still the wounded kept coming in their muddy, torn and bloodstained uniforms, often being laid out on along the Slopes to be stripped and cleaned up before being taken into the wards. So many were there that in 1915 the military hospital expanded into the second house of Cliff Terrace; by 1917 the whole had been taken over, as were the Pavilion and other large properties. The wounded were treated by local doctors and tended by St. John's Ambulance, Red Cross and VAD nurses. Occasionally, despite orders to the contrary, furtive men with the red tie and serge hospital uniform concealed by khaki greatcoat regaled themselves with honest English beer behind the Tankerton Hotel, the Royal, and in older pubs in the town below.

So Tankerton did its bit: throughout the war, young men grown prematurely old recovered from their wounds, learning, perhaps, to cope with lost limbs and gassed lungs in its bracing air.

Seeing their recovery convinced folk that a local hospital would mean they themselves would not need to make the jolting journey to the Kent & Canterbury Hospital. When the war ended, negotiations were rapidly opened with the military, and in April 1919 the ex-Military Hospital opened its doors to locals: in-patients were charged 3s. 9d a day; out-patients sixpence, and all were looked after by their own doctors. But with peace restored Mr. Fitt was eager to re-establish the Marine, and bought that half of the terrace occupied by the hospital. Patients now found beds at the former Pavilion Hospital while urgent fund-raising went on, culminating in 1926 with the opening of the new Cottage Hospital in Pier Avenue.

Meanwhile, great efforts were made to promote the delights of Tankerton-on Sea. The neglected roads began to fill with houses, shops extended along Tankerton Road, and a thousand-seater cinema, the Trocadero, opened. There was a bandstand, and the beach huts came back. For less well-off holiday makers, these were a boon: *'some are very artistic with their lace curtains, green plants, and a verandah that is a shade for the sun's rays'*. The huts were painted a variety of colours which made a happy sight against the background of the green slopes.

For the wealthier holiday makers of those halcyon days between the wars, Mr. Fitt's hotel provided 40 bedrooms, bars, billiards and a dance floor. There was even - sign of the times - a garage, and in private cars many a jolly excursion was made into the countryside and to Canterbury. The less well-off stayed in boarding houses with their own sitting room, or were content with board residence and trips by charabanc. The old Pavilion was refurbished and extended before emerging in 1936 as Tankerton's Café Royal - a hotel and a restaurant. Altogether it was a happy world of the seaside holiday. Games and deck-chairs along the slopes, family groups crowding the pebbly beach, donkey-cart rides, boat trips, concert parties outside the Tankerton Hotel, and always the wide panorama of sea, fishing boats, oyster yawls and cargo ships to please the eye.

It is an odd twist to the story which began with many like Herr Mohr who imbibed not wisely but too well, that Tankerton developed a sober image. The early trio on Marine Parade: the Tankerton, Marine and the Royal remain even today the only licensed premises. They somehow contrive to recall the twenties and thirties, when Tankerton finally came of age in a genteel atmosphere of health, wealth and recuperation.

Harbour Lights
Beach Road

Details of this building have not been found. It probably dates from around 1890 when this beach - then Tankerton beach - was the centre of Whitstable's seaside industry. The existing buildings were rather flimsy affairs of weather-board but this was the first one designed and built of brick. It was run as a cafe by Vittore Offredi, a well known caterer  in the town. Next door was built a large boarding house called 'Beulah', which then had very ornate wooden balconies. Later the two buildings were joined as the Continental Hotel, with the cafe part becoming the bar. Now the hotel section is in flats and the bar remains separate.

11 TALES FROM THE PUBS

Pubs depend much upon their landlords, or indeed landladies, for their character and reputation.

No publican, surely, can have been more popular and respected than Charles Taylor of the Steam Packet. When he died in 1888 in a yacht-racing accident, more than 1,000 people attended his funeral, mourning him as a 'friend, associate or helper'. He had collected money for the relief of orphaned children and developed a scheme whereby ships using the harbour contributed to the Kent and Canterbury Hospital and so entitled their crews to treatment there.

Some licensees held their tenancies for so long that they became institutions in the town. There was Harry Keam of the Neptune, who celebrated his

Rosie Gann - barmaid at The Railway Inn.

41st year there in 1893 by entertaining a party of 41 friends. There was a successor at the Neptune, Mrs. Phoebe Ramsley, who presided there from 1934 to 1974. She and her husband survived the war year with the beach outside festooned with barbed wire and an anti-aircraft gun and searchlight nearby. 'Regulars' remember her invariable response to 'Will you join me?' as 'I'll have a half of Guinness, thank you dear.'

However, it was not any Whitstable publican but a barmaid who achieved real fame, immortality even, as the principal character in one of Somerset Maugham's most admired novels 'Cakes and Ale'. Blackstable, the location of the early part of the story, is a thinly disguised portrait of Whitstable as the writer remembered it from his childhood. In the book he creates Rosie Gann, whom he makes a barmaid at the 'Railway Arms', and whom he surely based on a real barmaid in some *very modest little public house just opposite the*

109

Railway Inn
1 Canterbury Road

A small cottage opposite the Turnpike at the junction of Canterbury Road and Church Road (now Belmont), was bought by William Madams in 1845. Here his mother Emma opened a beer-house and this was continued by her son. Now William realised that this was a valuable position for by 1860 the railway line from London would pass immediately in front and the station would be opened on the bridge over the main road. William had already extended the original cottage along the Canterbury Road and now, mortgaging this property for £963 he added a very impressive public house front facing the railway: it was now the Railway Inn. He also converted another part of the cottage into a grocers shop. Then in 1866 he sold the public house to Henry William Madams, a ship owner on Island Wall and this paid off the mortgage. H.W. Madams died in 1879 and the Inn was sold to Flints, the Canterbury brewers, who had had an interest in the pub for some years. In 1888 the establishment was improved with a coach house, stables and a

new bar. It was here that the young Somerset Maugham glimpsed the bar-maid whom he immortalised many years later as 'Rosie' in his novel Cakes and Ale. So the Railway Inn has a real claim to literary fame! The inn prospered with the trade from travellers and railway workers until the station was moved in 1914. It continued however until the mid-1970s when it closed and became a private house.

station', which had *'a sort of sinister gaiety... on a winter's night as you passed by you saw men lounging about the bar,'* a fascinating sight to the young boy returning to the dull formality of the vicarage and his elderly unexciting uncle and aunt. Such glimpses stayed with him for years, haunting his memory until they emerged in what is regarded as his best novel. In it he writes of Rosie: *'there was a disarming frankness in her manner that put one at one's ease. She talked with a kind of eagerness, like a child bubbling over with the zest of life, and her eyes lit all the time by her engaging smile.'* And there was that other side to her character which both *'shocked and thrilled':* *'There wasn't a man who came in to 'ave a drink that she didn't carry on with. No matter who they was.'* How apt it is that Whitstable's claim to literary fame should thus feature the archetypal barmaid, surely based upon a real character. Who was she?

Of course some landlords fell on hard times, and some were not so popular. One such was the publican at the Ship Centurion, who in 1889, as the Whitstable Times reported, *'made an attempt to desert his craft, but, having failed to discharge his pecuniary liabilities, an opposition was launched in the shape of a formidable attack of snowballs which prevented the gentleman from leaving the carriage in which he was driven to the railway station; thus it came about that he lost the train by which he intended to travel, and consequently he was forced to resume his position "on board" until a more favourable opportunity presented itself... this we are informed occurred in the early hours of Monday morning, and the battered creditors, on renewing their demand for satisfaction, found the "Ship" with only a "centurion" in charge.'*

Ship Centurion (Ship)
High Street

This inn was first licensed in 1750 and was built by the Canterbury business of Fenner & Flint, coalmerchants and/or brewers. At that time it was really beyond the houses of Whitstable Street, as it was then called, and was doubtless built to capture trade from the passing waggons and travellers along the road to Canterbury. Behind the inn was a group of weather-board storehouses, a stable and a coalyard. The first inn keeper was William Waddington. 1801 it was sold to brewer Matthew Sankey and 1827 to George Ash, founder of the Dane John brewery. Edward Foad the landlord in the early 1800s had been partner with Nutt and Salisbury in the enterprise of building Island Wall and draining the Salts behind. Foad impetuously and against local advice, sowed wheat on his new land and the crop failed disastrously. So to recoup his fortune he took on the Ship. By 1845 it had become the Ship Centurian; the reason for this addition to the title is not known. Around the turn of the century the landlord was a well-known figure in the town: William Gammon, town crier (at 1/6d a time!). Like so many Whitstable publicans he was a former mariner: bos'un of the famous early steamship Great Eastern.

Local sailors on the east coast run would sing:
We crack on all our canvass, boys,
And for Whitstable town we sail.
And all the thought that's in our head
Is old Bill Gammon's ale.

The old building, low-ceilinged and several steps down from the street level, was demolished in 1914. As with so many new buildings in Whitstable at that time, the architect of the new Ship was A. A. Kemp. In 1923 ownership passed to Jude, Hanbury & Co of Wateringbury, and so by brewery amalgamation it is now a Whitbread's 'house'.

Many landlords were prepared to sail rather close to the wind on behalf of themselves and their patrons when it came to the law, especially in the little matter of Sunday drinking, for, from prosecutions brought in the 1860's and 70's it is clear that the local police were watchful for the illegal sale of alcohol on the Sabbath. Often they patrolled in plain clothes.

At the Cliff Cottage beer-house in Seasalter, for instance, the redoubted wife of the landlord was not to be put upon: she refused entry. *'Policeman or no policeman,'* she said, *'you're not coming in here.'* She claimed in court that she did not know he was a policeman and 'could not see his staff.' Whatever was going on inside her premises was protected; she was given the benefit of the doubt and the case was dismissed. But the long memory of the law prevailed. At the same hostelry eighteen months later, the constable had his suspicions aroused by furtive signals at the bottom of the hill, suspicions that were strengthened when the landlord tried to divert his attention by talking about seeds, and finally confirmed when he heard the landlord's daughter saying *'Here's the policeman: never mind your change.'* He then saw no less than fourteen men fleeing, leaving but one pot of ale upon the table: presumably they'd been passing it round. The landlord claimed the men were all hop-pickers *'who in pursuance of an old custom in the hopping season, every morning left their packs in his house for a carrier named Butcher to take on to the neighbourhood of the hop-fields'.* This appeal to tradition failed and he was fined £2 with costs.

Thirsty men, however, were not to be thwarted: a drink they would have on a Sunday. A Sergeant and a constable found a storehouse on the beach, its door fastened with string. Inside they found twelve men and five large stone bottles, three of which contained beer. The men and the landlord of the Guinea, who owned the storehouse and supplied the beer, were all fined. The same pair of officers conducted another raid two years later, which the Whitstable Times reported: *'Great satisfaction is felt by the respectable inhabitants of Whitstable at the step taken... to putting an end to the illegal sale of beer on Sundays.'* This time the target was a hut on some allotments. The officers, hidden one evening in the pig-pound, carefully watched the comings and goings. When a likely group had gathered to the sound of corks being drawn, the clink of money and the laughter of merry men, they pounced. Nine men were fined, but a link to the landlord of the Rising Sun was not proved.

When the law relented, and allowed drinking after mid-day on Sundays, still some earnest drinkers were not mollified. When caught at it too early, they sang: *'Down at the Rose in Bloom,/We all got there too soon./We felt so queer,/*

We had some beer/For which we had to pay too dear/Down at the Rose in Bloom.'

Sometimes landlords sailed a little too close to the law for safety: it was November 5th at the Pearson's Arms when Sgt. Gower called. As a result of what he saw the landlord was brought to court accused of running a disorderly house. The sergeant deposed that between 10 and 11 o'clock he heard the sound of fireworks. Upon entering the house he had found it full of smoke. The defendant inside was supplying the men with beer as fast as he could. He was warned he would be reported. Upon returning at 12 o'clock, Sgt Gower had found the same persons inside still letting off fireworks, some of the men having blackened faces, and others being drunk. The landlord was fined. With Whitstable's fire record it was as well the police were on this occasion vigilant.

There were too many pubs, that was the problem: custom was sometimes hard to come by and harder to keep. We shall see in Chapter Twelve that the number of pubs in the town caused concern to police and magistrates, and publicans might be refused a renewal of their license if strongly opposed by the police. Local magistrate Wynn Ellis once pointed out that there was one pub for every 120 inhabitants, and suggested that the Bench was not disposed to add to the number. Be that as it may, the Royal Native was refused as it was 'very badly conducted' and the landlord 'frequently got tipsy.' The Spread Eagle and the Horn of Plenty were similarly refused. The Wall Tavern was rejected at that time as 'devoid of accommodation': presumably just barrels of beer and standing room.

One publican at least was successful in renewing a license for the Prince of Wales. But, alas, he was in trouble before Christmas for 'suffering gaming by means of dice.' PC Bates reported that 'while outside the house he heard raffling for money going on,' and after listening for half an hour he entered the room and found several men engaged in raffling for pints of beer, but that on his appearance one of the men endeavoured to hide the dice by sitting on them. The law was patient as well as watchful.

Whitstable men were proud of their independence, and never took kindly to outside interference. The space outside the Duke of Cumberland, known as the Cross, was the traditional meeting place for the local community. Political meetings, religious services, protests and celebration - all were held here. Nearby, behind the inn, were once the stocks in which malefactors sat in disgrace. Summer evenings were sometimes the peaceful scene of Punch and Judy shows, lit by the light of one of the town's first gas lamps. But things were not always so tranquil.

A new Act came into force on August 24 1872 which required pubs to close at 11pm. *'The new arrangement came into force somewhat suddenly and it was received with dissatisfaction by a certain though not very numerous class, who railed against the government for depriving them of their liberty, and so on, and determined not to be done out of their beer, some of them took bottles of their favourite beverage onto The Cross and drank it there. For a time there was quite a commotion in the town, but it was of a harmless character.'*

By 1908, motor cars had appeared, and drivers complained that The Cross was too often obstructed by the Baptists with a harmonium and the Salvation Army with tambourines. The leaders of these two religious groups were duly charged and fined one token farthing, with eight shillings costs. Mr. Trevorrow of the Army refused on principle to pay and since he claimed to have no personal possessions he was sentenced to a day in prison. As he had been in court for a day, that was the end of the matter - except that the dreaded motor car had served notice of trouble to come. It seems that pedestrians already had to beware.

But horses prevailed for a time. It was from The Cross that many of the

---

Cliff Cottage Beer House
Admiralty Walk

This is mentioned in a court report of 1871 when landlord Stephen Hunt was charged with permit-ting Sunday drinking. Cliff Cottages were by the Coastguard Station. Stephen Hunt could well be the man of the same name at the Rose in Bloom, so maybe he also ran this little beerhouse for a very local trade.

---

popular Annual Outings started (for men only of course). Up until the Second World War no event was looked forward to with more anticipation than these junketings.

In July 1920, one Saturday, 25 members of the Guinea Club set of at 6 a.m.: *'The first call, for breakfast, was at 8.30 a.m., the rendezvous being the 'Queen's Head' at Boughton. On the way the company disembarked to give the horses a rest and walked through the charming grounds at Hernhill belonging to Squire Dawes. On arriving at the 'Queen's Head' most of the party proceeded to the garden and regaled themselves with fruit as an appetizer before breakfast... Justice was then done to a very fine cold meat collation with all the necessary vegetables and it was voted by all to have been a great success... the party then proceeded along the road to Boughton Lees, enjoying as they went a fine view of the countryside... Needless to say the party did justice to the refreshment that was carried as ballast... On arriving at the*

'Flying Horse' dinner was served and all agreed it was right good and well served by the host... Proceeding on the way a pleasant drive was enjoyed as far as Chilham where an excellent tea was served at 'The Alma', which concluded the programme as far as food was concerned... After tea the homeward journey was taken through Canterbury as far as 'The Ivy House' where a smoking concert was held and finished up a very enjoyable day's outing. The party arrived home about 11.0 p.m., all tired but unanimous in their praise.' And on suspects 'quite a bit the worse for wear', as they would have admitted.

Old Sportsman
Seasalter

There was originally a fisherman's cottage on this site which dated from 1642. It was owned for many years by the Fox family of Graveney. A later owner, Thomas Woolley of Faversham, was granted a license to sell ale in 1798 at the sign of the Sportsman. Around this time it may well have been involved in smuggling activities for which its lonely situation was most suitable. In 1814 William Court was landlord and then William Dunk, and his widow sold the inn to Shepherd Neame in 1888. Shortly after they built the main block of the present building, doubtless catering for the popular shooting parties which went out on the marshes. There was shooting of a different kind on 27th September 1940 when a German Junkers 88 bomber crashed not far away on Graveney marsh. Soldiers who dashed out from the Old Sportsman to take the crew prisoner found themselves met with a hail of bullets. The resulting battle is said to be the only one on the soil of Great Britain since the French tried to land in South Wales in 1792. The inn remains a Shepherd Neame 'house'.

It is a picture of some calm and much contentment, of an atmosphere that landlords encouraged, and one which we find in this description of the Stag around the 1880s: *'Could the walls of this house speak, what a tale they might unfold, of the cronies who used to make this their rendezvous practically every evening, for their game of whist. Their particular chair and corner reserved for the chosen few, the long clay pipes carefully put away the night previous with their respective ownership marks on them, the business of the village debated and commented on in solemn and dignified manner, the polished tankard containing foaming ale by their right hand, the ruling of the chairman when a knotty point arose, who, with clay pipe 'twixt finger and thumb, in a magisterial and judicious manner gave his decision, which was invariably accepted by this round table gathering... The old-fashioned time-piece in the far corner, its lustre dimmed by its age, whose hands sometimes pointed to 1.30 a.m. before it was decided to adjourn the discussion on what might have been the serious state of the working of the village pump. Then the homeward journey, dark as pitch, the fumble with the key, and then bed...'.*

But it is in the nature of things that not all drinking was as mellow and gentle as this. We saw in Chapter Four something of the problems the police had in maintaining order at some of the rougher pubs, especially those near the harbour. One such place was the Bricklayer's Arms, where, in January 1864 the police were called to eject a drunken seaman. His friends objected and a pitched battle followed, the seamen fighting with 'chairs, pewter pots, glasses, etc.' Four men were arrested, and in court it was said they were from Harwich. But if that made Whitstable men into angels, the effect was somewhat marred by the police observation that *'whenever a disturbance took place at Whitstable those liable to be called upon to aid the Police kept out of the way.'*

In 1872 the police were called to one of the pubs because of sounds of noisy music, dancing and singing. The constable found twelve men and three women: *'amongst the company being five organ grinders and several suspicious characters, including a convicted thief. The landlady was dancing with a prostitute'.* Riotous living indeed.

As was only to be expected, superior villainy was to be found at the Bear & Key. In 1872 a man, respectably dressed in every way as a gentleman, represented himself as a refugee from France, and stayed the night, *'faring sumptuously, not forgetting a glass or two of the best port after dinner.'* He slipped away the following day, the bill unpaid. A servant followed him and caught him buying a ticket for London at the station. The Station Master refused him permission to board the train, and the swindler airily made off towards Faversham. Mr Bourne, the landlord, followed him on horseback and observed him flitting behind a haystack. The worthy host went round the opposite way and apprehended the man. Having no money the malefactor was forced to leave some of his outer garments before being allowed to get on the last train to London. Later a maid at the Bear & Key found that her room had been entered, and some money and her new dress taken. *'On this discovery being made it occurred to Mr Bourne that when the Frenchman went away the hind part of his trousers was rather bulky.!'*

Trouble with other foreigners is recorded. Whitstable people love to claim uniqueness for events in the town. So it's an open question as to whether the only combat against the Germans on the British mainland really did take place on the marshes beyond the Sportsman pub. For, on 27 September 1940, as the Battle of Britain raged in the skies above, a German Junkers 88 bomber was shot down and managed to crashland, relatively undamaged, on Graveney Marsh. Irish soldiers billeted at the Sportsman rushed to the scene, and, according to the local account, a fierce gun-battle ensued for several hours until the crew surrendered. A celebrated episode of the TV series Dad's Army used the story-line. But another view is that the only firing was that of the German aircrew as they sought to destroy the intricacies of German technology before the enemy got their hands on it.

So, who knows? It's a good story which was doubtless told many a time in local pubs. There must be many more good tales of Whitstable and Whitstable characters waiting to be told to someone with time, a good tape-recorder - and a capacity for beer. A Whitstable native for sure.

12 FROM PAST TO PRESENT

The Beerhouse Act of 1830 allowed almost anyone to sell beer merely by paying a small fee to a remote Excise authority without having to appear before local magistrates. Whitstable was growing fast at the time, and many people set up new drinking places with little fuss. The lack of local records makes it very difficult for historians to identify and date them, at least until directories make an appearance.

In 1847 Bagshaw's directory named eight 'Inns and Taverns' and fourteen 'Beerhouses' in Whitstable. Kelly in 1862 named 21 'houses' and another eighteen beer retailers and so showed there were 39 licensed premises stretching from Seasalter through Whitstable to Swalecliffe. In 1869, all licenses had again to be approved by local magistrates, and 1895 we find the police opposing the renewal of the Nelson's licence on the grounds that there existed nine other houses within 200 yards and within 400 yards no less than twenty-five.

making application for a liquor license to the magistrates

But it was not only pubs that proliferated. Alternatives to them were appearing. The town was changing.

Until the middle of the Victorian period the 'functions rooms' of the larger inns were the only places where people could meet for public meetings and private celebrations. For example, the Duke of Cumberland's 'Large Room' not only accommodated the Oyster Freemen's annual Water Court, but had other uses. From an advertisement of 1814 we get a glimpse of its role as the local theatre. Here appeared Mr Gyngel 'the Eclipse of all Conjurors', accompanied in family tradition by Master Gyngel with a 'Pleasing Performance on the Slack Wire'. In addition to the 'Astonishing Sagacious Live Birds' and a concluding performance on the 'Musical Glasses' there were 'Optics' and the 'Microcosm' - a portent of entertainment to come. But the town was growing: chapels and the church appeared with attendant schoolrooms, the Music Hall opened in 1868, and people now had alternatives to pubs as meeting places.

119

The Music Hall was soon enlarged to become the town's Assembly Rooms and the focus of professional men: the affluent tradesmen, the shipowners, and the ship-builders. These were people for whom only the Bear & Key would have been considered in any way respectable. Within the growing town the artisan class, whose Friendly Societies had met in the larger inns also now found a new meeting place in the Foresters' Hall, opened by that Ancient Order in 1881. Previously it was a large private schoolroom, and today forms the main part of the town museum. Here 'Temperance' held sway and the emphasis was on family gatherings, concerts and teas. However the men's groups, such as sports clubs and the skittles league still met in the pubs, and these now became very much the venue for the working class. Here Thrift Clubs were often organised: tuppence to join and at least sixpence saved each week.

By the turn of the century there was national concern at the number of licensed premises. In urban areas there was at least one on every street, and in major cities they often existed cheek by jowl in rows. Opposed to this ubiquitous invitation to consume alcohol in large quantities was the powerful Temperance movement. So in 1902 a new Licensing Act was passed, giving magistrates even greater powers to renew licensed premises in relation to their number and character. The aim was to reduce the national total of 100,000 by a third.

In February 1903 the St Augustine's Brewsters Session received the police report on Whitstable. This pointed out that there were 46 licensed premises in the town, consisting of 33 ale-houses, 8 beer-houses, and five grocers and other off-licences. This averaged out at one to every 35 homes, or approximately one for every 41 adult males. In comparison it was noted that there were slightly fewer food-shops: twelve bakers, nineteen grocers and thirteen butchers - totalling 44.

Interestingly, during the discussions by the magistrates the comment was made that thirty years earlier, in 1873, there had been thirteen more licenses granted, which would have made a total of 54 - so proving the old saying: one for every week of the year.

As in the nation generally today, large breweries dominated: Flint & Sons of Canterbury (brewers, by local reputation, of 'Flint's Looney Broth') owned fifteen of the 'houses', and Shepherd Neame of Faversham owned the larger and more respectable ones. Four of the premises were owned by the Whitstable Ecclesiastical Charities, and only the Shades, run as a small family hotel, remained a Free House.

The Justices in the end 'referred for compensation', that is, for closure, only a small number. In 1906 the Stag on Sea Wall closed, as did the Hoy and the Shades, both of the latter being by now somewhat out of place in the prosperous High Street shopping area, followed by the Fisherman's Arms, Dredgerman's Arms, Royal Native and the Queen's Head. In 1911 the Brewery Tap in Oxford Street went, as did the Star far down Island Wall, and the Alma and the King's Head at the town end. All, it was said, were poorly maintained and little frequented.

When the Stag closed its pub fittings were put up for sale, and the details give us a clear picture of the simple character of a local beer-house. In its single bar there were two long drinking tables, one of birch and the other of mahogany;

Wheatsheaf
Herne Bay Road, Swalecliffe

A plot of six acres of ground in "Swalecliffe" containing two cottages can be traced back to 1705 when it was sold by Thomas Grigg to Charles Fairway, a mariner. 1746 he sold to John Blackman, a Whitstable blacksmith. 1806 the property was purchased by Andrew Hunt. During the 1830s the tenant Stephen Halliday established a beerhouse in one of the cottages. He was also a farmer. Then in 1840 he bought this, the Wheatsheaf, together with the other cottage and land, undertaking a mortgage for £800. Presum ably unable to cope with this Halliday sold for the same amount to George Ash, Canterbury brewer, in 1844. However he remained licensee and he was still there in 1862. Through amalgamation the pub passed to Hanbury & Co of Wateringbury in 1923 and six years later to Whitbread's, with whom it remains

The old building was pulled down in 1935 and replaced with a large roadhouse style public house at a cost of £8000. This was built back from the road with a large car-park in front. The licensee in 1940 said he could accommodate for supper meals 40 downstairs and 50 in the first floor room. The size of the new Wheatsheaf reflected a belief that the growth of Swalecliffe would produce a much larger volume of trade than has actually developed.

121

Just across the road was Kite farm and near the coast the Coastguard Cottages; presumably these supplied some thirsty men for customers. The first licensee was George Pout, noted in 1847, he was also an agricultural labourer; indeed the Pout family owned the nearby farm. The old building was bought by George Beer & Co, Canterbury brewers in 1900. By 1938 housing estates were beginning to grow in Swalecliffe and there were a number of tented holiday camps in Summer and so the brewery replaced the old Plough with a modern roadhouse style public house with a large car-park in front; it was called the Plough Hotel. However the trade anticipated did not really develop in Swalecliffe to justify such a large establishment. The Plough is now owned by Thorley Taverns of Thanet who renamed it in 1990 'Eddery's', after the well known jockey.

Eddery's (Plough)
Swalecliffe

This beerhouse was established in one half of an early nineteenth century cottage fronting on to the road. It stood in an isolated position out in the country on the winding lane which then linked Whitstable to Herne Bay. Although in the parish of Swalecliffe curiously the Plough and the large field behind belonged to the parish of Whitstable.

eighteen rush-seat chairs; 28 stamped pewter pint pots and four half-pints (obviously little call for the latter), and a quantity of glasses. Then there was the four-pull beer engine in a mahogany case with brass and porcelain pulls and brass taps, and that other important fitting: an eight-day clock in a mahogany case. It gives a picture of a very simple setting, but it was in such places that the tired working man found solace in gregarious company away from a cramped terrace house crowded with children.

The closures were a sign that times were changing: the general standard of living was rising, and people had higher expectations of their social venues. As often happens, the change was first apparent at the top of the social scale. It must have been in the 1870s that the Bear & Key acquired the facade we see today, accompanied by the dignified title of Hotel. The exterior of the Duke of Cumberland was remodelled in 1901 and its interior refurbished: *'The place has been thoroughly transformed, comfort being the sole aim... the billiard room is one of the best in the county, while the bars are excellently fitted with the most up-to-date appliances. One of the features of the saloon bar is a self-acting orchestrion, which is so constructed that twelve tunes may be played upon it, and the music is equal to that supplies by a full orchestra.'* Yet another precursor of modern pub entertainment had arrived: the ancestor of the juke box.

Change followed in lesser establishments. The ancient and dilapidated Nelson in Harbour Street was pulled down and rebuilt, as was the Ship Centurion, both doubtless to catch the trade engendered by the magistrates' closures. About this time the old smuggling beer-houses in the Seasalter countryside were rebuilt: the Sportsman (its lonely position surely reflecting a good trade in shooting parties), the Blue Anchor and the Rose-in-Bloom. Then, following the First World War, the decline of the harbour and the eventual closing of the old 'Crab & Winkle' line to Canterbury resulted in pubs in that area of town being put out of business.

In the 1930s, as housing estates extended from Tankerton into Swalecliffe, old country beer-houses were demolished and replaced with impressive brick buildings in the fashionable 'road-house' style: the Wheatsheaf and The Plough. Their swathes of asphalt car parks showing clearly that they were no longer relying purely upon local trade. In such a way the primitive Long Reach on Borstal Hill, of Fanny Wood fame, was 'translated' to a site on the concrete ribbon of the new Thanet Way: the carters of old replaced by the cars and charabancs of a newer age.

The motor car age also saw the decline of Whitstable and Tankerton as a seaside resort, especially after the Second World War. Today of the four sea-front hotels, only the Marine continues to offer accommodation. The other three have been turned into flats, though they keep their bars: the Harbour Lights (once the Continental), the Tankerton Arms, and the Royal.

Today Whitstable has 32 public houses or bars, and of these, no less than 28 date back to the Victorian period or even earlier: they are enduring features of the local scene. Some have been completely rebuilt, and all have been modernised to varying degrees. There are quite a number where patrons still perch around the bar to banter and gossip, with few concessions to comfort, they offer those essentials: beer and billiards. These are still very much the 'local' with their 'regulars', some of whom may have come for their daily beer for half a century or more. Many pubs are still very much social centres, even in this television age, with organised teams and evenings of entertainment. Most pubs have adopted an open-plan layout, removing that long-hallowed division between the 'public' and 'saloon' bars, and sweeping away those intimate corners in the 'snug'. For many the provision of meals is as important as the drink - they advertise now not the beer but the bar snacks and menus for full restaurant catering. Many public houses now provide the 'Sunday Lunch', a trend which is establishing the pub as a place for family gatherings.

Rather curiously in this modern age, a new image in style and decor often means an attempt to recreate the nostalgia of the past. Imitation beams and open brickwork, brass and bric-a-brac along the shelves and on the walls attempt to create an atmosphere of warmth, comfort and old-time companion-ship. Nowhere is this better seen than in the Long Reach, where the 1930s pub has been converted to a 'Beefeater Inn', an imitation olde worlde Tudor hostelry.

And so, 'curiouser and curiouser' as Alice remarked, the latest addition to our long list of Whitstable drinking places is yet the oldest. This, Chestfield Barn with its bars and restaurant, is indeed a most sensitive conversion of an old thatched manorial barn, occupying a site going back to at least the fourteenth century.

It is to be hoped that this book, likewise, will appeal to those who feel nostalgia for former days, and who, as they sip a pint or enjoy a meal, may like to know something of the background of their chosen pub, and to understand how it fits into the broad sweep of the history of the town. And for others who have yet to sample the special character of Whitstable there is the hope that they will feel the book has lived up to its introduction - that here have been good tales well worth the telling.

The Barn Tearooms - 1930

Chestfield Barn
Chestfield Road

The grouping of the great thatched barn and the adjacent farmhouse (now the clubhouse for the Golf Club) form a most picturesque reminder of earlier times when isolated farms with their attendant buildings and a cottage or two formed the only settlement in this area. This was formerly a lonely, isolated and scantily populated part of the countryside. The barn was part of Balsar Street Farm, taking its name from the family who owned it in the thirteenth and fourteenth centuries. Another family, of more knightly status, held the manor and their name - de Chestville - has survived as the place name - Chestfield. Traditionally the barn is known as 'Fourteenth Century', very likely the site, perhaps even some of the structural beams date from that time. The open countryside remained virtually unchanged down the centuries until Mr George Reeves bought Chestfield Manor and some 700 acres in 1920. Here, his passion for recreating timbered houses, his building skill and imaginative estate layout came together to create a new village. The barn at the centre of his scheme was utilised for many years as picturesque tea-rooms, for Mr Reeves was teetotal and would not permit a public house in his vision. Later on it became a restaurant and finally in 1988, after a major renovation and reconstruction of the interior, Chestfield Bar became both the newest and yet on one sense the oldest public house-cum-restaurant in the area. It is a 'free house'.

Bibliography

Whitstable History:

1. Goodsall, Robert 'Whitstable, Seasalter and Swalecliffe - The History of Three Kent Parishes', Cross & Jackman, Canterbury 1938.

2. Hart, Brian 'The Canterbury & Whitstable Railway', Wild Swan Publications Ltd., 1991.

3. Hasted, E. 'The History and Topographical Survey of the County of Kent' 2nd. Edition in 12 vols. 1797 - 1801, edition E.P. Publishing Ltd. 1972, - 'Seasalter - Whitstable - Swalecliffe' vol. 8.

4. Harvey, Wallace 'Whitstable and the French Prisoners of War' 1971; 'The Seasalter Company - A Smuggling Fraternity (1740 - 1854)' 1983; 'Seasalter and the Mystery of Robinson Crusoe' Emprint Publications, Whitstable 1989.

5. Hollingshead, John, journalist author not attributed in 'All the Year Round' edited by Charles Dickens; 'The Happy Fishing Grounds' 26.11.1859; 'Another Whitstable Trade' (Diving), 14.1.1860.

6. Igglesden, Charles 'A Saunter through Kent With Pen and Pencil', Vol. II, pp. 21-56, Kentish Express, Ashford 1914.

7. Page, Michael '"Grit in the Oyster" - Somerset Maugham's Formative Years in Whitstable and Canterbury', Whitstable Improvement Trust n.d.

8. Pike, Geoffrey 'The Story of Copperas and the Castle', Whitstable Improvement Trust 1991.

9. Pike, G.; Cann, J.; Lambert, R. 'Oysters and dredgermen', Compass Publications, Seasalter 1992.

10. West, Douglas 'Portrait of a Seaside Town - Historic Photographs of Whitstable' in four books published 1984 - 1991, Emprint Publications, Whitstable.

11. Whitstable Times - on microfilm at the town library: from 1864 to the present day.

12. Woodman, George and Greta 'We Remember Whitstable', 2nd. Edition, Whitstable 1988.

Licensed Premises

Clark, Peter 'The English Alehouse - a social history 1200 - 1830', Longman 1983.

Moncton, H.A. 'A History of the English Public House', Bodley Head 1969.

Victualler's Recognizances - under an Act of 1552 victuallers were required to give two recognizances for character and good behaviour at Petty Sessions. Annual bundles of these survive from 1649 - 1749 (KAS Maidstone Q/QLv1) but they refer only to West Kent. However from 1723 - 1773 annual lists for the St. Augustine Division survive recording all victuallers with their inn signs (KAS Q/RLv3). Thus only scanty references to inn-keepers occur for Whitstable before 1723. While the lists after 1773 give the victualler's name only, this presents no problem for Whitstable as down to 1830 the same eight inns continued:

Bear	Ship
Duke of Cumberland	Two Brewers
Hoy	Blue Anchor
Red Lion	Monument

The Beer-house Act 1830 - alarmed at the prevalence of gin drinking, the Government sought to make beer more widely available by allowing any householder to set up a beer-house solely on the purchase of an Excise license, without the requirement to appear before the magistrates. This was only restored in 1869. So after 1830 the beer-houses proliferated and no direct record of their establishment is available. By 1861 there were 33 in the Whitstable area and the number continued to grow (see Chapter 12). Dating of the establishment of the beer-houses has often had to be inferred from property deeds, directory entries and the Census returns (unfortunately those for 1841 are missing)

Acknowledgements

The following are most gratefully thanked for their assistance in the preparation of this book:

1. Mr. Wallace Harvey for material from his archive and personal information.

2. Shepherd Neame at the Faversham brewery for deeds of public houses.

3. Whitbread Plc. at the Fremlin brewery, Maidstone, for public house deeds.

4. Deeds of individual properties: Mr. D. Annis; Mr. D. Bird; Mrs. E. David; Mr. B. Green; Mr. B. Packham.

5. Mr. G. Laurens for the Blue Book Directories.

The correction of information given in this book, or access to additional sources, especially deeds for former public houses now private houses, will be greatly welcomed by the researcher Geoffrey Pike.

INDEX

Licensed premises - inns, pubs etc. - are only noted in the Index if references are made in the text. The full guide to all known premises is shown on the inside back cover.

128

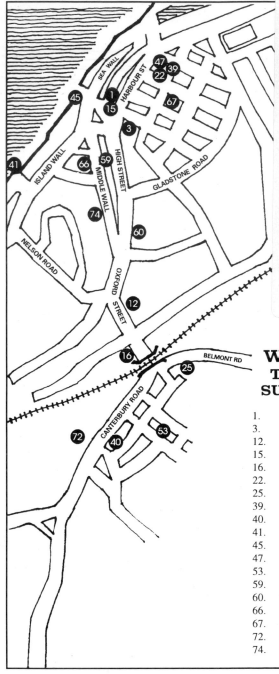

WHITSTABLE
TOWN CENTRE
SURVIVING PUBS

1.	ALBERRES
3.	BEAR & KEY
12.	COACH & HORSES
15.	DUKE OF CUMBERLAND
16.	EAST KENT
22.	FOUNTAIN
25.	GOLDEN LION
39.	NEW INN
40.	NOAH'S ARK
41.	OLD NEPTUNE
45.	PEARSONS ARMS
47.	PUNCH TAVERN
53.	RISING SUN
59.	ROYAL NAVAL RESERVE
60.	SHIP CENTURION
66.	SMACK
67.	SOVEREIGN
72.	TWO BREWERS
74.	WALL TAVERN